Cameos of t
Salient P

Flanders and Picardy 1914 -1918

by Tony Spagnoly
and Ted Smith

with an introduction by
Keith Seldon

LEO COOPER

By the same group of authors in The Cameos of the Western Front series:
The Anatomy of a Raid
Australians at Celtic Wood, October 9th, 1917

Salient Points One
Ypres Sector 1914 - 1918

A Walk Round Plugstreet
Ypres Sector 1914 - 1918

Salient Points Two
Ypres Sector 1914 - 1918

Poets & Pals of Picardy
A Weekend on the Somme with Mary Ellen Freeman

A Haven in Hell
Talbot House, Poperinghe

First Published in 2001 by
Leo Cooper/an imprint of Pen & Sword Books Limited
47 Church Street
Barnsley
South Yorkshire S70 2AS

Content © Tony Spagnoly, Ted Smith and Mary Ellen Freeman 2001
Introduction © Keith Seldon
Maps © IMCC Ltd.

Front cover design by Ted Smith from an idea by Jim Ludden

A CIP catalogue record for this book is available
from the British Library

ISBN 0 85052 790 2

Typeset by IMCC Ltd. in 10.5 point Garamond Light.
Printed in Great Britain by
Redwood Books Ltd., Trowbridge, Wilts.

CONTENTS

DEDICATION

To David Ross
2nd South African Regiment
Wounded at the age of 13-years and 9 months,
September 1917 at Zonnebeke, Ypres Sector
Died of wounds in enemy hands
at the age of 14-years and 3 months, March 1918
at Gauche Wood, Cambrai

And in the end of course
War is never about war
But it is about Love and memory
And, it is about sorrow

The Things They Carried
Jim O'Brien

ACKNOWLEDGEMENTS

We would like to give thanks to all who helped in any way in the compilation of this book.

Special thanks go to Terry Bishop, Lieutenant-Colonel Parmley, Steve Potter and staff of The Keep Military Museum of the Devon and Dorsets, Dorsetshire for an endless source of information and photographs on the Dorsets, to Rhian Edwards at Wrexham Library for searching and supplying a list of almost impossible-to-find books, to Peter Barton of Parapet Productions Ltd. for his direction on the mines at Messines, to J. Clifford Williams for his invaluable information on Adolf Hitler, to the late Don Forsythe for research undertaken in South Africa and to David Cohen of David Cohen Fine Art for his help with information on the artist Edmond Carlos.

Pat Freeman deserves a special vote of thanks for making available a wealth of information for use with the Michael O'Leary story as does Gotrand Callewaert for being more than forthcoming with his knowledge on the 1918 actions at Neuve Eglise. Likewise a big thank you to Marcel Leplat who, for his collection of postcards, should be awarded the title of 'The Plugstreet Postcard King', and Christian Carpentier for his help and co-operation with on-the-spot digital scanning of the said postcards at his computer premises in the square at Ploegsteert. Our gratitude also extends to Claude Verhaeghe, proprietor of L'Auberge, the restaurant opposite the Ploegsteert Memorial, for the use of his e-mail facilities to get the postcard scans sent to Ted Smith's computer, and thanks also to Nelly, Claude's wife, for supplying Ted with countless cups of coffee, a few of which she let him pay for.

Patrick Roelens and his work with the Société d'Histoire de Comines-Warneton helped clarify a great deal of the mystery around Le Gheer, Le Pelerin and 'Plugstreet' Wood with his profound knowledge of the area and Bril Emmanuel and his research activities in the Bailleul and Meteren areas, was extremely helpful on the Neuve Eglise actions.

Although not the norm to thank the writer of an introduction to a book, special consideration and thanks in this case is given to Keith Seldon in Brussels who was almost bullied into taking on the task at very short notice.

As always the staffs of the Imperial War Museum, the Commonwealth War Graves Commission and the Public Record Office pitched in with their usual, enthusiasm, patience, knowledge, and co-operation and for that we are truly grateful.

Most of all, our acknowledgements go to the men, both those who fell and those who survived, that endured the hardship and suffering of the Great War.

Mary Freeman, Ted Smith and Tony Spagnoly, August 2000

INTRODUCTION

I was asked to write an introduction to this book mainly because I have spent many years researching the long-term effects and influences on the cultures of populations that have lived under the occupation of an aggressor and the attitude of those populations in peacetime, both to the invading nation, and to those responsible for the eventual and inevitable liberation. The nature of this work has caused me to spend much time in France, Alsace Lorraine, the Malmedy and Eupen areas of north-west Belgium and of course those other areas in Flanders and Wallonia of Belgium that were under occupation during the years 1914 to 1918.

I was asked to read as a 'study course' three other books in the *Cameos of the Western Front* series. Of the authors, other then Ted Smith whom I have known for over thirty years, I know little. Tony Spagnoly I once met when he visited Brussels, Mary Freeman I have never met but have had the pleasure of reading her book *Poets & Pals of Picardy*, and the anonymous contributor of the Michael O`Leary V.C. story is known only to Ted Smith.

What struck me about the books was that they are clearly not written about 'invaders' or 'liberators', but about individuals and their involvement in war, intentional or otherwise. This should not have surprised me as the concept of this series has been clearly stated a number of times but, in my experience however, book series habitually claim to major in-depth on a subject, and generally fall short of it.

With this book, *Salient Points Three,* I was particularly impressed with the quotations at the head of each opening chapter, all relevant to the subject of the cameo. Credit goes to Mary Freeman for the search and selection of the quotations and to the other authors for accepting her recommendations.

The variety of the writing styles adds dimension and interest to the individuals, the events and the areas in which they took place. Tony Spagnoly`s treatment of *A Soldier for a Year, An Artist at War* and *Adolf Hitler* is emotive and perceptive, verging on the spiritual and of what could have been, while Mary Freeman with her sensitive and appreciative feeling, coupled with an all-embracing knowledge of the men, their characters, families, friends and background brings to life Captain Jack Pixley in *A Very British Grenadier,* Lieutenant Julian Grenfell in *Into Battle — Julian of the 'Ard 'Ead* and the officers and men of the 1st Battalion the Dorsetshire Regiment in *No Prisoners for the Dorsets*. 'Mr Anonymous' brings much more to *The Wild Colonial Boy* than the courageous events leading to Michael O'Leary's being awarded his Victoria Cross. What he and the award meant to the people of Southern Ireland together with its political connotations brings a different angle to a dramatic story. Ted Smith with his work on the Duke of Cornwall's Light Infantry at Hooge and Ypres in *Triumph and Tragedy,* the exploits of the different tanks and their commanders in *Tanks at St. Julien,* and the efforts of a corporal in the Machine Gun Corps and the officers and men of the Worcestershire Regiment in *Corporal McBride and the Worcesters at Neuve Eglise* concentrates on the drama of military action and the reactions of men to the confusion and the unexpected turn of events in combat, while his appraisal of the *Five Forgotten Mines of Messines* leaves me in some doubt as to whether I would ever want to visit the area around Le Pelerin or La Petite Douve Farm in southern Belgium.

Whereas the book did not convert me towards becoming deeply interested in the events of 1914 to 1918, it did move me, and cause me to think and to reflect on what armies, formations, aggressors, occupying forces, military machines and other descriptions of the like really are. It brought to mind that, although a large proportion of the men employed in such organisations at the time were professionals, for the better part they were ordinary men wearing similar uniforms and doing a specific job for a short time. It seems few of them actually saw the enemy and none of them were prepared for what they were to experience. Few realised, while spending a particular day in a foreign country in a muddy ditch suffering a bombardment of shells, awaiting an order to attack a pile of soil and bricks situated on the other side of a field smothered in barbed wire, that they were in fact playing a part in this or that offensive, were the first wave of an attack opening the Battle of X, Y or Z or were to be the first of many to suffer the effects of poison gas or some other hideous weapon. And the man relaxing somewhere with a few friends when a stray shell blew him to pieces won himself a soldier's grave, not a hero's death. Simply the penalty for being in the wrong place at the wrong time.

The book also prompted thought on the casualty figures related to battles. I've read before of the 100,000 here, 50,000 there and in smaller actions: 12 officers killed, 125 other ranks killed, wounded or missing. Now each one of those numbers represents a man to me, a loss to someone — mother, father, uncle, aunt, brother, sister, son or daughter, and, no matter what, merits more than being just one of the sum of a casualty figure. If anything, *Salient Points Three* has caused me to think of the soldier, not as a well-trained, efficient but faceless and essential unit of a country's military might, but more as a person, part of a family and a social circle, just like me and mine. He spent time, and maybe fell, in places I visit and through this book I can follow in his footsteps.

The format of the book I found to be agreeable and informative, leaving me with a different aspect on many of the places that I have visited in the course of my studies. When next in those areas I will be well aware of some of the events that took place thereabouts and of those individuals who passed that way before me. I will certainly make the effort to find the time to tread the paths and visit the sites, made all the more easy for me by the maps at the opening of each story. That alone interprets my praise for the efforts of those who put together this book.

Keith Seldon, August 2000

There is a saying, much used in the advertising business, and I'm sure in other sectors of industry, which states "There's never time to get it right, but always time to do it again". With the wealth of information available on the Great War, and with the vast number of organisations in place to help in delivering it, the Public Record Office, the Commonwealth War Graves Commission, the Imperial War Museum, military museums and libraries as well as national, family and personal archives, sited throughout Great Britain with their counter-parts in other countries throughout the world to start with, it is difficult to understand why so many publications are produced containing incorrect information. "Getting it right" should be fairly simple – but it isn't. A good proof-reader is worth double his or her weight in gold, and finding one will ensure the elimination of spelling and grammatical mistakes and the odd 'typo', but research, research and more research is the only answer to getting 'it', the facts and chronology of events, in order. But professional research teams are hard to come by, and expensive too, and anyway, when do you stop researching? The answer of course is never, but that doesn't bode well for the book publishing industry or the person trying to earn a living as a non-fictional author. So research cut-off time is down to the judgement of the author or editor when it is believed that all avenues have been exhausted, or by the publisher who has a bill to foot and a print schedule to meet. But who judges the judge?

How many authors rely on the research of their contemporaries for information on their own works and, in so doing, compound the error of another? How many enthusiasts of the Great War are walking around believing something to be true which is, in reality pure, fiction? Those who have read *Salient Points One* might believe that the Lost Mines of Messines are lost, when in fact their positions are well recorded and available for all to see. Likewise the position of the Messines mine that exploded in 1955. Do people believe that its position was as shown on the map featured in that particular cameo when in truth it exploded in a field on the other side of the road? At the time of publishing it was believed by the authors to be the case, but further research and information from others who know better has proved otherwise.

I remember being assured by a battlefield tour guide that the circular lawn at the entrance to the Hooge Crater Cemetery was the site of the original Hooge Crater. Another informed a touring coach party that one of the three craters now forming decorative ponds in front of the Hooge Château of today was also the Hooge Crater. Neither was correct, but how many present on those two occasions believe what they were told?

Another time I was given a copy of an article from an issue of the *Ypres Times* published in the 30s talking of *The Lost Platoon*, the 16 men of the 6th Duke of Cornwalls Light Infantry buried in the Ypres Reservoir Cemetery who were found in the St. Martin's crypt after the Armistice. I used this piece as part of a presentation when acting as a tour guide for one of the Major Holt's tours and have since found it to be just another myth, supported nevertheless by the cemetery register. How many people now believe that one? It would be fairly safe to presume that something written for the *Ypres Times* in the 30s by someone who had served, with support from a C.W.G.C. cemetery register, would be a fairly safe bet, but it isn't. Likewise with the action of the 2nd Worcesters at Neuve Eglise? Their superb history, published in1928, talks about their battalion headquarters in the town Mairie. It recounts the story of Captain Crowe's V.C. being won in the adjoining fields. What adjoining fields? There are none, nor were there any in 1918. It mentions the gallant actions of men firing over the Mairie garden walls. What garden walls? The Mairie doesn't have an accessible garden, nor did it in 1918. All this is down to an error, a very acceptable one considering the conditions at the time, when the town Hospice was mistaken for the town Mairie. The war diaries at the Public Record Office carry the same information. This understandably incorrect information also highlights the fact that others at the time relied on the writings produced by contemporaries for their own works. *The History and Memoir of the Machine Gun Corps* and Lieutenant-Colonel Seton Hutchison's *The Thirty-Third Division in France and Flanders 1915–1919*, published in 1919 and 1921 respectively, carry the same mis-information as the Worcester's history. Lieutenant-Colonel W. D. Croft in his *3 Years with the 9th Division*, another 1919 publication, made some real whoppers when talking of events of the Royal Scots, and a map-reference mentioned by R. B. Talbot Kelly in his excellent *A Subaltern's Odyssey* (1980) is very misleading although, again, understandable. Another excellent regimental history, *Historical Record of The Buffs (East Kent Regiment) 3rd Foot, 1914–1919* (produced in 1922) completely threw me when researching and producing the map covering their 6th and 8th Battalions' involvement in the history's recorded attack on Spoil Bank. The spoil bank they attacked was never officially called Spoil Bank, nor is it the one shown on military maps as Spoil Bank, although not too far away from it.

So what to do? One way is to be open to criticism and the good-will of others who choose to point-out mistakes. Whether he did it by intent or not, Peter Barton of Parapet Productions Ltd., pointed me in the direction of the Royal Engineers' map at the Public Record Office showing the exact positions of the abandoned mines at Messines, which I was convinced nobody knew about. I certainly didn't.

Another way is to get out to the battlefields, check the maps study the ground, and meet with and talk to people of the local communities. No less than 15 Belgians chose to inform me that the 1955 mine exploded in the field opposite to the one I indicated on the map produced for the Messines cameo, and it was Gotrond Callewaert, a native of Neuve Eglise, who indicated that a machine gun operating from the first floor of the Mairie could not have been, and that the building thought by the Worcesters to be the Mairie was in fact the Hospice on the hill to the north of the town square.

So if anyone who happens to read this book has any information that will help to "Get it right", do everyone a favour and contact me.

Ted Smith, September 2000

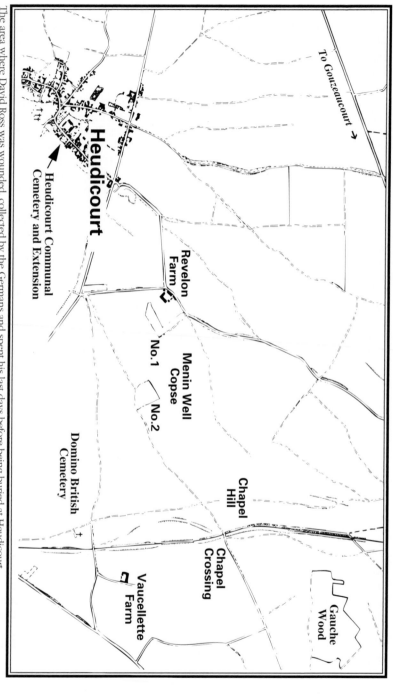

The area where David Ross was wounded, collected by the Germans and spent his last days before being buried at Heudicourt

Youth in its flush and flower
Has a soul of whitest flame,
Eternity in an hour,
All life and death in a game.
Lieutenant W.N.Hodgson

1

A SOLDIER FOR A YEAR
Private David Ross, 2nd South African Regiment
Frezenberg and Heudicourt 1917–1918

WHEN 700 SOUTH AFRICANS emerged from the hell of Delville Wood in July 1916, they had lost over eighty percent of their active strength, but had won imperishable glory and a place in history for the South African soldier. Following this action the general view of the military authorities was that the South Africans would be hard put to play a full part in the general operations that followed the summer campaigns on the Somme. However, this view was quickly overturned when the South Africans replenished their numbers with base volunteers, a return of the lightly wounded and the transfer of trained men from the homeland. They soon added to their reputation with actions at the Butte de Warlencourt in October 1916, where they suffered an ill-affordable 1,152 casualties, and again in the Arras offensive of April 1917, where once more they proved their worth.

By the time the brigade moved north to fight at Third Ypres in September 1917, another batch of much-needed young reinforcements had arrived to fill its ranks. Having enlisted in the February of that year, these recruits had received only minimal basic training, so badly were they needed. One of these arrivals, serving with the 2nd South African Regiment, was 13-year old David Schalke Ullundi Ross from Durban, Natal. Not much is known about his early life, but it must be assumed that he was a mature boy, mature enough to convince the recruiting sergeant on 5 February 1917, that he was old enough to join the army, having signed-on as 18-years and 6-months old. Whatever the case, the authorities were satisfied, and with the South Africans in dire need of every man they could get, all volunteers were gladly accepted.

On enlistment, his personal details were entered as 5ft 7⅝ inches in height, chest 38 inches, with heart and lungs in good order and religion given as Church of England. He was of dark complexion with black hair and blue eyes. The authorities were satisfied, with his given age and the foregoing, together with his signature, was all that was required. The 2nd South African Regiment had a new recruit, Private No. 11322D. S. U. Ross. He was now part of that elaborate machinery of war which would draw him to the Western Front. No parental approval seemed to have been needed. He was born in Durban in January 1904, his father, Colin George Ross, was of Scottish ancestry and his mother, Sarah, was of Afrikaan descent, thus giving young David the Afrikaans 'Schalke' portion of his name. 'Ullundi' would appear to have been given to him after one of the British victories over the Zulu nation which had swept this far-off province of the British Empire.

David listed his mother, Mrs Sarah Ross and 10-year old brother Colin, as his dependants, ensuring them an allotment from his pay. It is not known whether his mother knew what her elder son was up to, and the thought of him having taken himself off to war might have horrified her. Whatever the case, David Ross was on his own, a fully signed-up member of the South African forces. Three weeks later he was with a replacement draft aboard the *S.S. Walmer Castle* heading for the battlefields of Europe, disembarking at Rouen on 22 May.

The 31st found him with the 2nd South African Regiment, then operating with the 9th (Scottish) Division. The division was at rest following its efforts east of Arras in the April, complementing the Canadian attack north at Vimy Ridge A further period of rest took place in the area of the Somme, where minor raiding and strengthening of the line was the order of the day. Here Ross was indoctrinated into battalion life and front-line trench experience. This was a quiet time for the division as it prepared for the summer battles then being planned for Flanders. It would not be too long before the British offensive at Messines in June 1917 paved the way for the beginning of one of the world's most historic battles, Third Ypres, better known as the battles for Passchendaele. The South Africans would soon be on the move, and the young David's baptism of fire would be upon him.

The battles were nearly two months old when the South Africans arrived in Belgium to play their part. Their big day would come with an attack on 20 September 1917, an attack on a line with all the advantages in favour of the enemy defenders. The Germans were secure in their deep redoubts and behind the thick walls of their pillboxes, sited in the many ruined farms and homesteads that lay on the plain before the village of Zonnebeke, itself guarding the lower reaches of the ridge which led to the Passchendaele heights, the ultimate objective. Capturing Zonnebeke would afford the British an observation platform which could unhinge the German defences further north.

The 9th (Scottish) Division would attack along the line of the Ypres–Roulers railway with the many German fortified pillboxes sited along its length. The South Africans would dispose on the left of the line, moving in the general direction of the Bremen Redoubt. with the 27th Brigade to their right. The 2nd Australian Division would cover the 9th's right divisional flank and 55th (Lancaster) Division their left, securing the heights of Hill 37, heavily defended by a network of forts.

The days leading up to the 20th had been subjected to persistent rain, and the ground was sodden and flooded in parts but, at dawn on the 20th, the drizzle was replaced by a clinging mist, impeding visibility. Hence David Ross's first view of an actual battlefield was not a very favourable one, and he might have thought at the time that perhaps he was not quite as mature as he had supposed, wondering what lay before him. A heavily-flooded obstacle, the Hannebeke stream, confronted them, supported by pillboxes already spitting machine-gun fire. The Hannebeke had ceased to flow, its banks blown by months of relentless shelling, its course marked by a zig-zag of shell-holes, deeper and more water-filled than the others. Trenches and belts of thick wire around the Bremen Redoubt would present another major problem as visibility began to improve with daylight. Accurate German artillery fire monitored by observers on the heights was making life difficult for the attackers, and the prospect of getting into the correct take-off positions across the slippery muddy ground proved to be a dispiriting exercise. However by the allotted time of 7 a.m. they were in position to move onto their first main objective, the line running north and south in front of Mitchell Farm, a German strongpoint since May of 1915, and then onto the second, a line straddled by Waterend House and the Bremen Redoubt, two major strongpoints on the outer defences of Zonnebeke.

Despite the unfavourable conditions, the attack developed well. The Scottish infantry moved along the line of the railway and attacked the great bunkers of Potsdam at the heart of the enemy defences. The Lancastrians had problems along the heights of Hill 37 to the left, unable to prevent sweeping machine-gun fire from Pommern Castle on the crest and Tulip Cottages at the base of its southern slopes, being laid-down on the advancing South Africans. Nevertheless, the strongpoint complex of Berry Farm and Beck House fell quickly to the infantry of the 4th South African Regiment. The 2nd Regiment, under the temporary command of Major Cochrane, leap-frogged through their lines, past the smoking ruins of the first objective, heading for the second, the Waterend Farm–Bremen Redoubt sector, with the Hannebeke, Mitchell Farm and Zavenkote to contend with on the way. In the murky darkness, enemy machine-gun fire was ripping across the plain, causing the South Africans heavy casualties as they struggled across the Hannebeke.[1] Somewhere between the stream and Mitchell Farm, David Ross took a severe gunshot wound to his left leg.[2] He fell to the sodden earth, his brief experience of the dreaded Ypres Salient coming to a speedy conclusion. He had come 800 miles for about five minutes of infantry action before being carried, wounded, from the battlefield. So ended David Ross's brief involvement at Ypres. Never more would he return to this place which had exacted such a price from the 2nd South African Regiment – 61 killed and 224 wounded in an action that had lasted only a couple of hours.

In spite of heavy casualties all along their line, the division's attack was a resounding success. The two major objectives on the South African front were wrapped-up, the enemy retreated to new positions north and east of Zonnebeke, Potsdam fell after some particularly heroic individual actions, and the Lancastrians had finally wrenched Hill 37

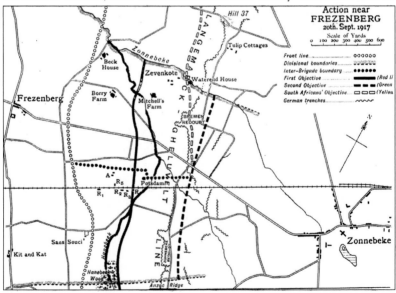

The strongpoints and objectives of the action on 20 September 1917

from the reluctant grasp of the Germans. The day's battle had cracked open the enemy defences in this area and, although the advance was limited, and the haul of 3,000 prisoners had often been bettered, few battles had been fought more bitterly for an area of land which comprised no more than a mass of quagmires, destroyed farms, shattered pillboxes, splintered copses and overlapping, water-filled shell holes[3] – but this desolate morass had been of vital importance to the enemy defences and was now of equal importance to the aspirations of British High Command.

Young Ross was carried to the main collecting post near Potize Château before being ferried by ambulance through Ypres to No. 32 Casualty Clearing Station at Brandhoek, where he would receive more intensive attention. His wound was serious enough to see him, within 48 hours, leaving Brandhoek, travelling on the medical rail link that fed the hospitals on the French coast. From there he was transferred to No. 22 General Hospital on the south coast of England, where his damaged leg slowly recovered. From here he sent a postcard to his mother not daring to say too much and making out an allotment to her of fourteen shillings a week. Knowing where her son was, and why he was there, it is hard to believe why his mother made no effort to have the young warrior brought home. He stayed in England until the dawn of 1918, the last year of his young life. 12 February 1918, found him fit and well, back in France at the Infantry Replacement Depot, Rouen, on the way to rejoin his regiment.

When he eventually caught-up with the 2nd South African Regiment in March, it was defending Gauche Wood, a small woodland on a ridge just south of the village of Gouzeaucourt and the southern extremity of the old Cambrai battlefield, helping to plug a gap during the German onslaught of that month. It was 21 March and the great German offensive designed to split the Allied armies was about to begin. Gauche Wood was directly in the path of several German storm-trooper divisions, The enemy came smashing through, pushing everything before them as they made advancing inroads into the 16th (Irish) and 21st Divisions either side of the South Africans defending the wood. Time and time again they came, only to be repeatedly thrown back with terrible losses caused by the concerted rifle and machine-gun fire of the South Africans who, likewise, were incurring tremendous losses. It was a virtual massacre, as Corporal Williams of the 2nd Regiment put it: "I was at Delville Wood but. I have never seen such bloodshed, and nor can I have imagined such losses".

The German elite were being pushed back on their heels, and each time they launched a new attack, they had to climb a barricade of their own dead to get into the flaming woodland, so fierce was the fire of the South Africans. One Wurtemburger of the 123rd Grenadiers, when once more pushed back to the start line between the wood and Villers-Ghislain, was recorded as saying "To us Grenadiers, it was a miserable situation. We felt ashamed and shattered".

Eventually the battered South Africans moved out of the Wood allowing the dispirited enemy to occupy it. The Germans had taken enough punishment and did not venture from the protective edge of what foliage was left, knowing that, if they did, the ever watchful South Africans in the cluster of buildings at Chapel Crossing to their west, and those on Chapel Hill, a small hillock nearby, would bring a fierce fire to bear. As the smoke of fierce battle lifted from the wood and the

David Ross's Casualty Form

surrounding battlefield, the Germans gathered-up the dead of both sides and buried them in mass graves in and around the wood.

David Ross had been wounded within the wood, his final movements unknown. His wounds must have been serious enough for him to have been picked-up by the enemy and carried off to Revelon Farm, equipped as an Advanced Dressing Station by the British, and later used by the Germans when they took over the sector for the same purpose. He was reported as missing on 24 March and a day later, 25 March, two days after the South Africans withdrew,[3] the young South African, a soldier for a year, died in enemy hands at the suspected age of 14-years and 2-months. His grave can be found today in the small communal plot behind Heudicourt village church, then a short stretcher-carry away.[4] Two other British soldiers are buried alongside him. He was one of the youngest British soldiers to die in the Great War.

In the absence of any evidence to the contrary, John Condon, Royal Irish Regiment, killed in action at Ypres in 1915 and now buried at Poelcappelle, must be the strongest candidate for that most poignant of titles 'The youngest soldier to die in the Great War'. He was 13-years and 11-months old when death took him at the end of the Second Battle of Ypres. David Schalke Ullundi Ross was only three months older. Both boys lie at rest, sharing the same light, and are surely bonded in that most unique brotherhood, the one of eternal peace. Long may their joint memory be honoured.

Notes:

1. The Hannebeke Stream was often referred to as the Steenbeek which it ran into at its northern end near St. Julian.

2. Lance Corporal William Hewitt. 2nd S.A. Regt. won a V.C. attacking a bunker near Mitchell Farm on 20th September 1917. He died in 1966.

3. Traces of the Potsdam complex and smaller pillboxes remain along the course of the old railway embankment, now a road from Hellfire Corner to Zonnebeke.

3. The remnants of the Brigade were pulled back on 22-23 March to Heudicourt, leaving behind David Ross, one of their 2,000 casualties of the action

4. A larger plot of 85 British graves concentrated from other local burials lies close to the site of David Ross's grave. The Aid Station position at Revelon Farm can still be seen from the village church. The ground around Gauche Wood is in much the same condition as it was in the Great War. In the wood itself trench lines are easily recognisable; Chapel Crossing is still there, although all the buildings have long since gone, and Chapel Hill is still a part of the landscape.

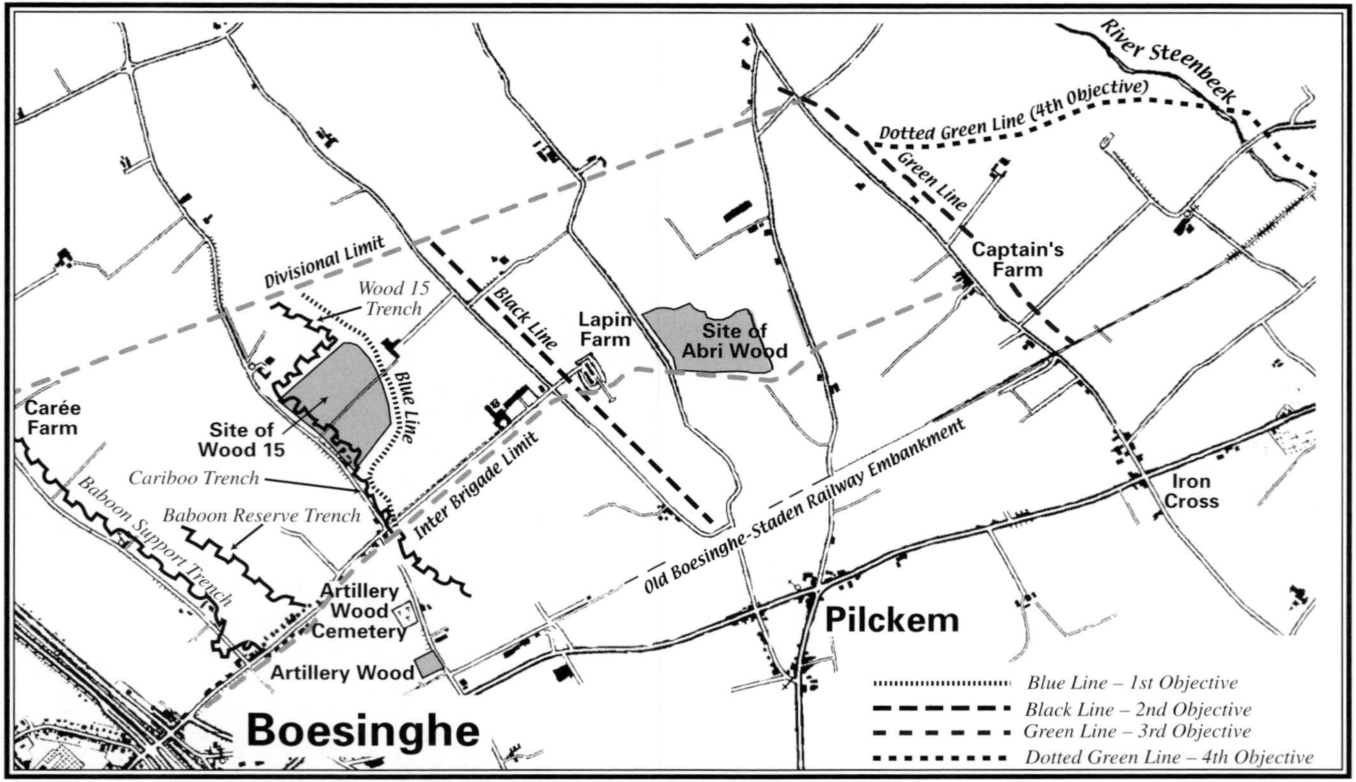

The Guards Division operations on 31 July 1917, showing the points where Captain Jack Pixley saw action

Map labels:

Carée Farm
Baboon Support Trench
Cariboo Trench
Baboon Reserve Trench
Site of Wood 15
Divisional Limit
Wood 15 Trench
Blue Line
Boesinghe
Artillery Wood Cemetery
Artillery Wood
Inter Brigade Limit
Black Line
Lapin Farm
Site of Abri Wood
Old Boesinghe-Staden Railway Embankment
Pilckem
Green Line
Dotted Green Line (4th Objective)
Captain's Farm
River Steenbeek
Iron Cross

Legend:
.... Blue Line – 1st Objective
– – – – – Black Line – 2nd Objective
––––––– Green Line – 3rd Objective
• • • • • Dotted Green Line – 4th Objective

8

God's in His heaven,
The Guard's in the line.
The Guardsmen's motto -
a parody of Robert Browning's 'Pippa Passes'

2

A VERY BRITISH GRENADIER
Captain J. N. F. Pixley, 4th Battalion Grenadier Guards
Boesinghe Sector, Ypres, Belgium 31 July – 12 October 1917

A RTILLERY WOOD CEMETERY at Boesinghe in Belgium, a small village just east of the Yser Canal a few miles north of Ypres, is the last resting place of two Great War poets, Hedd Wyn and Francis Ledwidge. Opened as a burial plot by the Guards Division after the opening of the Battle of Pilckem on 31 July 1917, this British military cemetery also houses the last mortal remains of a Captain of the 4th Battalion the Grenadier Guards: John Nicol Fergusson Pixley, killed in action near Houthulst Forest on 12 October, 1917, during the battles for Passchendaele.[1]

Born in 1888 into a wealthy family, Captain Pixley, known to friends and family as Jack, was the second eldest of four brothers and three sisters whose father, Colonel Francis Pixley, was a stockbroker and Knight of the Order of St. John of Jerusalem.

Not much is known about Jack's early life other than his attendance at Hawtrees, a private preparatory school in Margate, an area popular in those days for the boarding school education of the privileged. From there he entered Eton in 1901 at the age of thirteen. College records show that he only stayed three years, being prematurely superannuated in 1904 at the age of sixteen. There is then a gap of three years during which it would seem he received private tuition in order to prepare him for entering Oxford. In October of 1907, he entered Merton College where he read for a Pass Degree in Political Economy. Then, in 1912, an old Etonian and Oxford friend Denys Finch-Hatton, a prospector in Kenya, suggested Jack leave his employment in an architect's office in Oxford and join him in British East Africa in order to set up in partnership.[2] This was a very exciting time, as opportunity and expansion beckoned in hitherto unsettled foreign climes, and, full of enthusiasm for the life and fortunes of the enterprising settler, Jack sailed for Africa and a new life.

In a memoir of her mother, Nellie Grant, niece of the Duke of Westminster, the writer Elspeth Huxley provides an insight into the life of settlers in British East Africa at this time. In Nairobi, the conditions encountered were primitive, with people living outside the city fetching provisions by ox-cart, and most accommodation, even in the city, consisted of rudimentary dwellings with outdoor pit-latrines. Jack and Denys settled on a house in the city itself, near the well-known Norfolk Hotel, described by their mutual friend Julian Grenfell as "a palace" where they would "entertain the countryside on champagne and caviare". The house soon became the focal meeting-place for people of social standing and eminence who were settling in East Africa at the time. Nellie Grant, who had recently emigrated with her husband Jos, stayed with Jack in June 1913 having travelled by mule-cart to attend an Old Etonian dinner and the King's Birthday Ball at Government House. Nellie comments on the respite it provided from the usual standard of accommodation and also at the numbers of young eligible bachelors at the time.

Following the death of his brother Jocelyn, Jack was under a certain amount of pressure as heir to the Pixley estate, to adhere to the more conventional path of his contemporaries back in England, but still elected to stay in the Protectorate in spite of finding the place not wholly suited to his sensibilities.

Although he wrote in a letter to one of his sisters, Olive, how 'unpsychic' British East Africa was, Jack developed a love for big game hunting and, in the evenings, the pleasure of card-playing, one of his favourite pastimes for which he was nicknamed 'Lucky Pixley', a name that was to follow him into the trenches of the Western Front. Life in this outpost of the British Empire was a world away from the privileges of British high society. Elspeth Huxley describes the effect of the outbreak of war on this somewhat removed world:

> With radio yet to be invented, no telephone and mails that took up to six weeks each way, people were encapsulated in their small world. The shock was all the greater when it came. But one day a telegram came, collected by Nellie at Thika post office: "Nothing doing, European war expected." It sounded unbelievable. Back at Kitimura, Jos and Nellie played a game of tennis on the newly made court. A neighbour sent a series of chits from across the river: "Vienna Bourse closed. Troops mobilising. War inevitable." Exasperated Jos scribbled on the back of the last chit to arrive "What war?" And finished the set.[3]

The outbreak of war signalled sweeping changes to the old British Empire. Jack, like many other settlers, joined the East African Mounted Rifles as a Trooper just four days after war was declared. As a young man in search of adventure, Jack saw this as an opportunity to change the unfocussed path he was following, and grasped it with relish. In Nairobi everything was in confusion, with settlers converging upon the Norfolk Hotel with horses and rifles, not knowing quite what to expect from the German settlers just across the border in German East Africa. However, most of the fighting Jack encountered consisted of minor 'scraps' and the defence of important railway and transport thoroughfares.

Back in England many of his friends had already seen considerable service on the Western Front, some of them, such as the Grenfell brothers and John Manners, cousin of the illustrious Coterie 'darling' Diana Manners, were already dead.[4] Duff Cooper, later to marry Diana, was a close friend of Jack and suggested that he return to apply for a commission in the British Army. Jack's service in East Africa had lasted nearly a year when, in the summer of 1915 he was made an Esquire of the Order of St. John at the request of his father and in the ensuing Autumn he returned to London where his family were preparing to relocate to a large country house at Wooburn in Buckinghamshire. His request for a commission was granted and he became a Second-Lieutenant in the 4th Battalion Grenadier Guards, Special Reserve of Officers, although his training was delayed due to the effects of bouts of fever which debilitated him throughout 1916 and allowed him to spend time with the family in their new residence.

Wooburn House was an imposing and comfortable country home, with Jack's big game hunting trophies adorning the ornate walls of the grand entrance and hall.[5] His niece remembers visiting the family, and fondly recalls playing hide-and-seek with Jack and one of his friends. Jack shared a special bond of siblingship with one of his sisters, Olive, who relates their story in a brief but fascinating account entitled *Listening In, A Record Of A Singular Experience* which focuses on their continued relationship after Jack's death through psychic communication.[6] One of the many walks in the grounds of Wooburn House ran alongside the river in the direction of the church and was a favourite of Jack and Olive where they spent a good deal of time together, sharing their thoughts. It was an idyllic time, but such times would not last indefinitely and, after six months, on 1 January 1917,

Captain Jack Pixley was posted to join the 4th Battalion, then part of the 3rd Brigade, Guards Division, at Mericourt on the Somme, northern France.

Officers were welcome reinforcements for a regiment that had sustained heavy losses in the September fighting of the Somme Offensive the previous year.[7] In early 1917 the Guards Division were involved in general duties between Combles and Peronne where, after March, it was engaged in the construction of roads and railways to help facilitate the British advance in the wake of the German retreat to the Hindenburg Line. However, mid-June saw it move into billets at Herzeele farther north, just west of the Franco-Belgian border where it remained for two weeks before moving across the frontier into the Boesinghe sector of Belgium in early July. During this period at Herzeele the Division was in serious training for the Battle of Pilckem scheduled to open on 31 July, the first of the eight battles to take place between 31 July and 26 October, collectively and officially known as Third Ypres.[8]

Troops arriving in the notorious Ypres Salient in mid-1917 were confronted with a very different landscape from the one encountered by the British Expeditionary Force in the October of 1914. The landscape encircling Ypres had deteriorated into a muddy morass, with the front line just a series of linked shell holes across a terrain extremely difficult and dangerous to negotiate. The war correspondent Philip Gibbs encountered such conditions when he arrived in the Salient in July, describing them as the 'hell of Flanders':

The condition of the ground, out from Ypres and beyond the Menin Gate, was partly the cause of the misery and the filth. Heavy rains fell and made one great bog in which every shell crater was a deep pool. There were thousands of shell craters. Our guns had made them and German gunfire, slashing our troops, made thousands more, linking them together so that they were like lakes in some places, filled with slimy water and dead bodies. Our batteries, as often I saw them, were stuck in the mud up to the axles of the wheels. Our infantry had to advance heavily laden with their kit, and with arms and hand-grenades and entrenching tools – like pack animals – along slimy duckboards on which it was hard to keep a footing, especially at night when the battalions were moved under cover of darkness. If a man were wounded and fell off a duckboard into one of those water-logged craters, he drowned in it.

The 4th Battalion's camp, a bivouacked area in a wood due west of

Boesinghe, was well within the range of enemy artillery and, apart from regular shelling, it was constantly experiencing gas alarms. Oliver Lyttleton, later Lord Chandos, had been in the 3rd Battalion until mid-June 1917 when he was promoted Staff Captain, 2nd Guards Brigade. He describes the Guards Division sector in his memoirs:

On June 10th we heard that we should make the critical assault on the extreme left of the British line, and next to the French Corps, the *Corps de Fer.*

The Boesinghe Canal divided our front line from the German: the ground was flat for a thousand yards behind the enemy position, it then rose gently to Houthulst Forest. There were numbers of farm houses turned into strong points in the enemy defensive system in depth. Moreover, we were under direct observation from the Pilckem Ridge and the whole of our forward communications round the village of Boesinghe and back to Elverdinghe were overlooked. It seemed a tough task, and our chief concern was how to cross the canal. The bed of the canal was about seventy feet wide, and except for a small stream of water which ran down the middle, was filled with soft mud, in which a man sank quickly. The German trench ran along the Eastern bank."

Divisional Headquarters determined that the Guardsmen would have to make their crossing of the canal over:

... narrow mats with wooden cross-pieces: a hand-rail was to be rigged so that when the mats were below the water level a man could guide himself across. The Royal Engineers also constructed a number of light pontoon bridges, supported by petrol tins, which were to be run across as soon as a few men had gained the other bank.

On 16 July the 4th Battalion had moved near the front and then, on the 18th advanced into the front line, taking considerable artillery fire in the process. Jack Pixley's No.1 Company took up position in the fire trenches edging the west of the Yser Canal, with the remainder of the battalion dispersed in support and reserve trenches. On the 20th, raids were made on the enemy lines in eight different places. At 1 a.m. on the day, Jack's raiding party started off well enough but found the mats laid to help them across the canal, at this time of the war a shallow drift of wet slime, were too short and the men had no option but to jump into the canal and struggle across it, knee deep in slime and mud. They managed to enter the German trench in the right place but the raid wasn't very successful, being terminated when one of the raiders dropped a bomb, killing his neighbour and wounding himself into the bargain. Nevertheless, the information gleaned by the raiding parties overall indicated that the enemy only held his front line in posts, regularly withdrawing its garrison at dawn to concrete dug-outs and pill-

A Guards' carrying party crossing the Yser Canal by a duckboard bridge

14

boxes in rear of the line to avoid shelling, leaving the trenches lightly guarded and supervised by not too frequent patrolling parties.

Reports from overflying British aircraft confirmed the observations of the raiding parties, adding that the front line trenches were frequently unoccupied for days on end. On 27 July, taking advantage of the situation, the Divisional Commander set up a superb impromptu action – the 3rd Battalion Coldstream Guards crossed the canal in broad daylight, with no supporting artillery, and entered these front line trenches, quickly taking prisoner the few light German garrisons holding them.[9]

Captain Lyttleton explains the re-adjustment of battle plans as a result:

At night we patrolled the canal vigorously and soon found that the front trenches opposite were always lightly held and sometimes evacuated altogether. In broad daylight a battalion of the Coldstreams crossed the canal and gained a foothold, which was rapidly extended. The French came into line on the left of the 3rd Guards Brigade, and because the 38th (Welsh) Division on our right could not advance, we threw out a defensive flank. The attack now seemed to be of a more conventional character, but still looked tough.

With the Guards Division's attack frontage now on the east of the canal, a difficult crossing had been eliminated along with undoubted heavy casualties that would have accompanied it. Further to this, the seventeen bridges thrown across the canal, now to the rear, would provide assistance and safeguard communications.

Field-Marshal Haig later stated that this action had:

Greatly facilitated the task of the Allied troops on this part of the battlefront, to whose attack the Yser Canal had previously presented a formidable obstacle.

Jack and the 4th Battalion had been relieved on the 23rd by the 2nd Scots Guards and withdrawn to Battle Area Camp where they remained until the 31st, moving in the very early hours back into the line, rested and ready for the 3.50 a.m. attack. The British barrage opened, signalling the start of the Battle of Pilckem. The barrage was an awesome spectacle and battle experience for those taking part in it. Described as the heaviest British barrage of the war, Captain Lyttleton noted:

We had never heard or seen anything to match it. On that morning it

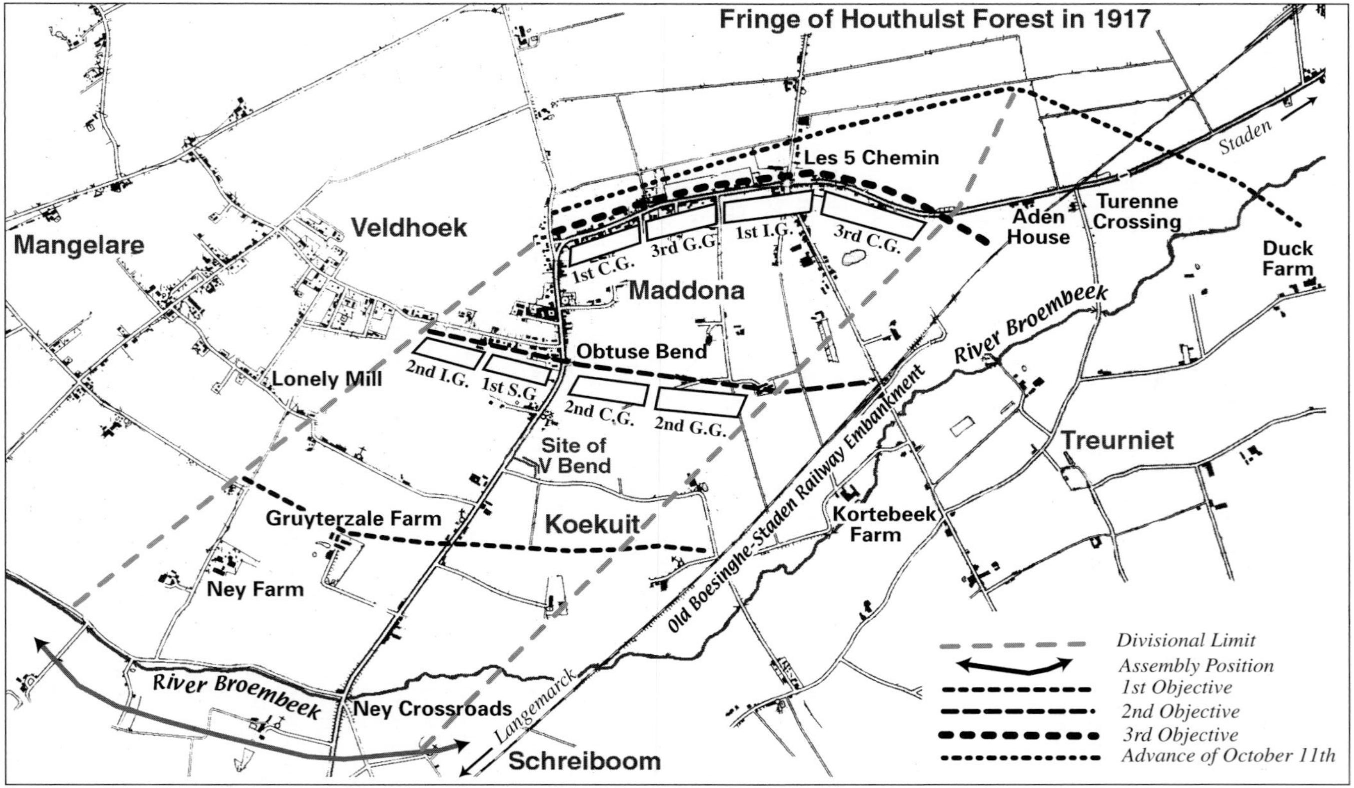

The Guards Division positions and objectives on 11 October 1917

Mangelare

Veldhoek

Fringe of Houthulst Forest in 1917

River Broembeek

Ney Farm

Ney Crossroads

Schreiboom

Langemarck

Gruyterzale Farm

Lonely Mill

Koekuit

Site of V Bend

2nd I.G.

1st S.G.

2nd C.G.

Obtuse Bend

Maddona

1st C.G.

3rd G.G.

2nd G.G.

1st I.G.

3rd C.G.

Les 5 Chemin

Old Boesinghe-Staden Railway Embankment

Kortebeek Farm

River Broembeek

Treurniet

Aden House

Turenne Crossing

Duck Farm

Staden

Divisional Limit
Assembly Position
1st Objective
2nd Objective
3rd Objective
Advance of October 11th

16

was said that £18,000,000 worth of 18-pounder ammunition was fired: the whole sky flickered with the flame of the discharges, and the enemy lines appeared to be drenched with the explosions of salvo after salvo. We had to wait for the 38th Division to get into line and then advance. This was achieved in perfect order, but the left flank of the 38th were held up by some pill-boxes and heavy machine-gun fire.[10]

Jack Pixley, having already accompanied Lieutenant-Colonel Lord Gort, the 4th Battalion's Commanding Officer, up the line to inspect the trenches from which the Battalion would attack, was now, with his No.1 Company, moving forward under the barrage, following the 1st Grenadiers whose task, with the 1st Welsh Guards, was to take two set objectives, the Blue and Black lines. The 4th Grenadiers and the 2nd Scots would then move through these two battalion lines to take the 3rd objective, the Green line.

With the heavy enemy shelling, the noise and the semi-darkness, the 4th's attacking companies, No.s 1 and 4, lost direction, finding themselves mixed with Grenadiers, Irish and Scots Guards south of Artillery Wood, a small woodland just north of the Boesinghe–Staden railway embankment. Despite the lack of landmarks and a considerable amount of hostile machine gun fire, Jack soon re-formed his company and re-directed them, following the 1st Battalion toward Wood 15, a large wood in the centre of the enemy support trenchlines, a sector of the Blue line, and then on to the Black line. It then passed through the 1st Battalion lines, being held up temporarily by the moat around the fortified Lapin Farm, before entering Abri Wood, another pill-box infested stretch of woodland blocking their way onto their objective. They successfully cleared the wood then attacked and captured a strongpoint called Captain's Farm in the Green Line. Their objective well taken, they began consolidating the line. Jack had just selected a concrete dug-out in the Captain's Farm complex as his headquarters when he was requested to hand it over to be used as the 1st Battalion's Headquarters. He had hardly left it when it was destroyed by a direct hit. He then moved his quarters to a nearby hut, but had to leave that when the 1st Battalion took over the whole line. Soon after, the hut was demolished by another direct hit. What with the raid of ten days earlier and two close shaves on the 31st, he was already living up to his nickname of 'Lucky Pixley' and, later in the day, he was promoted to Captain.

The next day, 1 August, the 4th Battalion was relieved by the 3rd

Battalion Coldstream Guards and went into rest camp near Poperinghe.

Throughout August it spent various periods in and out of the trenches south of the River Steenbeek. September saw it moving from camp to camp before, on the 21st, moving back to Herzeele, where it stayed for three days before returning to Penton Camp near Langemarck in Belgium. It remained here until 5 October, working both in the front line trenches and as carriers for material to the supply dumps preparing for the forthcoming Battle of Poelcappelle, scheduled to open on 9 October. The weather had taken a turn for the worse and Jack Pixley's sector, being at sea-level, was badly affected. The banks of the River Broembeek, one of nature's obstacles to the successful movement of the attack, had been breached and were horizontally diffusing water through the top soil with the men engaged in laying mat-crossings over the marshy swamps to enable troop movement to be effected without harassment of heavy, mud-clinging labour. On the morning of the 7th, Lieutenant-Colonel Viscount Gort, again with the now acting-Captain Jack Pixley with his escort, took representatives of the 1st Guards Brigade to inspect these mats that their battalions were to use. On the night of the 7th, after a day of torrential rain, the 4th Battalion retired to Dulwich Camp near Bleuet Farm, a dressing station west of Boesinghe, on the road to Elverdinghe.

All that remains of the 'pill-box infested' Abri Wood

At 5.20 a.m. on the 9th, the Guards Division crossed the Broembeek and attacked northward. The 4th Battalion was not involved in the launch attack, its duty being to hold the current line with the rest of the 3rd Brigade. It had moved into the line near Wood 15, the men lying in shell holes and abandoned gun pits in the pouring rain for the next two days. On the night of the 10th, the brigade moved up to the take over the newly consolidated front, relieving the attack brigades. Jack Pixley's company now found itself holding a section of the line at Vee Bend, a cluster of German pill-boxes on a small road with an acute angled turn just east of the road running north out of Langemarck on its way upward through Houthulst Forest. The relief took place under extremely heavy shelling and in the most atrocious of conditions, described as:

... a mass of shell holes full of water with the sides of the front line slipping and crumbling.

Men were expected not only to consolidate such positions but patently to launch attacks from them across the quagmire in front of them and, indeed, to all sides. Relief operations were just as arduous. as in order to reach men in the front line it was necessary to negotiate this appalling terrain and, for a good part of the time, under heavy enemy bombardment. Good logistics are the key to any successful army and subsequent battle manoeuvres and it is a measure of the fortitude and endeavour on the part of men fulfilling this task that troops in forward positions were able to operate at all. Even bringing up rations became an operation of the most enormous difficulty and magnitude, one which the companies were finding increasingly arduous and time-consuming given the nature of the ground to be traversed.

On the 11th, battle orders for the following day were received. The attack objective was to move the whole line northward to within 150 yards of Houthulst Forest. This forest had been occupied by the enemy since October 1914 and was now a veritable fortress, destined not to be taken from them until late September 1918. At 5.25 a.m. on 12 October, the attack was launched, the opening of what was later officially entitled First Passchendaele. As soon as the creeping barrage moved forward, two platoons of No.3 Company advanced behind it, capturing their objective with comparative ease. Two platoons from Pixley's No.1 Company moved forward to occupy the vacated front line in close support. The advance incurred minor casualties, with the Germans offering little resistance. At about 11.30 a.m. the enemy's barrage ended, and the rest of the day proved uneventful, with none of the expected counter-attacks taking place.

On the night of the 13th, after seven consecutive days in the open, including two days in bivouacs on the east of the canal, exposed to the rain, lying on heavily waterlogged ground with little or no shelter, and taking part in a major offensive, the 4th Battalion was relieved, and after making its way back to Boesinghe, entrained to Ondank sidings, north-west of Elverdinghe, where it went into billets at De Wippe Camp. Its total casualties in the operation were 20 killed, 4 missing, and 64 wounded.

'Lucky Pixley', the 4th Battalion's charismatic young aristocrat whose promotion to Captain was confirmed on the day of the opening of the attack did not travel with his battalion to De Wippe Camp. On 12 October, whilst moving up to the line to inspect his two platoons manning their forward trenches, Jack had been killed by one of the many enemy snipers left behind to harass the British advance. His body was taken back down the line to the Guards' burial plot just north of Artillery Wood where it was laid to rest.[10]

Men of the 4th Battalion at a captured strongpoint just south of Houthulst Forest

Within the space of just under three months he was buried in the sector where he first saw action, and in the very area from where he re-directed his No.1 Company back into the attack line at the opening of the Battle of Pilckem.

At Artillery Wood Cemetery, Jack's headstone reflects the thread of continued existence as experienced by his sister Olive who carefully chose the inscription from St. John's Gospel:

What I do thou knowest not now; but thou shalt know hereafter

Captain J. N. F. Pixley
4th Grenadier Guards
*Captain Pixley is buried in Artillery Wood Cemetery,
Boesinghe, Ypres, West Flanders, Belgium. XI. C. 5.*

Jack was laid to rest amidst the strains of shell and shrapnel, which was in itself a more dignified farewell than many who died here. However, every night at Ypres, under the Menin Gate on that well-trodden pathway to the Salient – the Menin Road, the bugles sound *Last Post* for each one of the multitude of men whose lives were so abruptly extinguished and who now lie in Flanders' fields and their cemeteries. This is always a moving event in this emotive place where the last note of the soldier's requiem lingers breathlessly on the Flemish air. Stephen Graham of the Scot's Guards details the significance of this most poignant of sounds:

The Last Post is the Nunc Dimittis of the dead soldier. It is the last bugle-call. As you stand in heavy cloaks about the new-dug grave in which the dead comrade is lying, it seems as if in a sepulchral way he also must hear it – as it were the last voice of all earthly, persistently, persistently calling. It is the last, but it gives promise of reveille – of the great reveille which ultimately the Angel Gabriel ought to blow.

Artillery Wood Cemetery, Boesinghe

Notes:

1. Artillery Wood Cemetery was used as a front line cemetery until March 1918. At the Armistice it held 141 graves of which 42 belonged to the Royal Artillery. The bulk of the remainder belonged to the Guards Division. It was enlarged by the concentration of 1,154 graves from around Boesinghe and now contains 1,295 war graves. Around 50 of the Guards' graves were originally sited in Captain's Farm Cemetery, a burial plot at the German strongpoint where Jack Pixley handed over his dugouts just before they were demolished by direct hits.

2. In her memoir *Out of Africa*, Baroness Karen Blixen writes of her love affair with Denys Finch-Hatton, portrayed in the motion picture by Meryl Streep and Robert Redford. Denys Finch-Hatton, second son of the Thirteenth Earl of Winchelsea and a noted member of the Eton-and-Oxford set, was killed in an aeroplane crash in 1931. A memorial bridge dedicated to him in the grounds of Eton was designed by the architect Sir Edwin Lutyens.

3. Jos Grant served during the war in the Royal Scots being invalided from active service as a result of wounds from a hand grenade on 5 November 1915 whilst in the Ypres Salient. Nellie's brother, Captain, the Honourable Richard Eustace Grosvenor, Royal Field Artillery, was killed in action in October and is buried at Vermelles British Cemetery near Bethune, France.

4. Lieutenant, the Honourable John Neville Manners 2nd Battalion Grenadier Guards, was killed in action while directing the fire of his platoon at the cross roads at Rond de la Reine in the forest of Villers-Cotterêts on 1 September 1914, and is commemorated on the La Ferté-sous-Jouarre Memorial just north of Paris, France.

Jack, although on the fringe of *The Coterie*, nonetheless had links with many members of the Group. The mother of Diana Manners, Violet – the Duchess of Rutland, was herself a member of a close circle of friends *The Souls* which included Margot Asquith, Charlotte Ribblesdale, Ettie Desborough, Mary Elcho and Francis Horner – all of whom were to lose sons in the war. Their residences provided the setting for country week-ends and dinner parties where a network of warm friendships grew up between the women and their families, the children of which formed the close friendships that later evolved into the *Corrupt Coterie*. Duff Cooper, a civil servant at the Foreign Office, was integrated into *The Coterie* by way of his friendship with John Manners. Duff joined the Household Brigade, 3rd Officer Cadet's Battalion, on 5 July 1917, entraining at Bushey Park initially before being attached to the Guards' Brigade and being posted on active service in April the following year. He finished the war as Second Lieutenant A. D. Cooper D.S.O, 3rd Battalion Grenadier Guards. Apart from being awarded the D.S.O. he was also Mentioned in Despatches.

In a letter to Duff Cooper, Diana mentions hearing the news of Jack's death from Osbert Sitwell in the middle of attending the opera. Jack was undoubtedly one of her suitors though it seems that it was mostly out of a sense of guilt that Diana felt so upset at his death:

> Jack Pixley has been killed. It upsets me a lot. My endurance is weakening. Osbert told me as he often does – a great ill-omened bird – in the middle of the

opera, and I have come home and cried and been beastly to Mother on the subject of my lovers, which O shame! comforted me .... I am so sad about poor 'Lucky Pixley' and for the first time in my life a little more remorseful that I wasn't nicer and didn't come up from Chirk two days earlier though he begged me to. If only one happened to know Death's plans.

Although Jack had not been conventionally religious, the family arranged a memorial service for him on 28 December, 1917, at St. Martin-in-the-Fields which was attended by many of his friends who were home on leave.

5. After the death of Jack's parents, his mother in 1932 and his father in 1933, Wooburn House, built in 1756, stood empty until it became Fenton School in 1937. The school failed and closed in 1938. In 1939 the house became home to the Commonwealth War Graves Commission. The Commission re-located in 1962 and, in 1963, Wooburn House was demolished to make way for Wooburn Manor Park.

6. *Listening In, A Record of a Singular Experience.* By Olive C. B. Pixley,. Copyright:– *Armour of Light Trust Council.* Olive had planned to join Jack in Nairobi as housekeeper in the summer of 1914 but, due to the untimely intervention of the outbreak of war, neither she nor Julian Grenfell – also due to join Jack and Denys at this time, were able to realise their plans. Olive commented: "How seldom do the Golden visions of youth ever materialise!"

7. Two such fatalities from the fighting on the Somme were Lieutenant Raymond Asquith, son of the Prime Minister and Margot Asquith, who died of wounds on 15 September 1916, and his relation by marriage, Lieutenant, the Honourable Edward Wyndham Tennant of the 4th Battalion Grenadier Guards who was killed in action 22 September 1916. He was sniped while firing at the enemy with his revolver from a communication trench called Gas Alley in the trench system in front of Lesboeufs, Somme, France. Both Guardsmen are buried in Guillemont Road Cemetery, Somme, France.

8. Third Ypres 31 July–10 November 1917.

The battles during this period are officially named:

i.   Battle of Pilckem, 31 July–2 August.
ii.   Battle of Langemarck 1917, 16–18 August.
iii. Battle of the Menin Road, 20–25 September.
iv.   Battle of Polygon Wood, 26 September–3 October.
v.   Battle of Broodseinde, 4 October.
vi.   Battle of Poelcappelle, 9 October.
vii. First Passchendaele, 12 October.
viii. Second Passchendaele, 26 October–10 November

9. Major-General G. Feilding, the Guards Divisional Commander, conceived the plan of seizing the canal in broad daylight without the aid of an artillery barrage. He took the chance that the absence of the Germans from their forward trenches would not be only momentary. Orders were given verbally to Lieutenant-Colonel Crawford commanding the 3rd Battalion Coldstream Guards who sent out strong patrols, closely followed by supporting platoons of moppers-up, to fixed objectives on the

western side of the canal. The Germans were taken completely by surprise and were made prisoners. So quickly and unobtrusively was the raid carried out that the Germans in rear were totally ignorant of what was happening in front. In the next few days, as German patrols entered their front line for a supervisory check, they too were made prisoner.

10. The Lyttletons were a highly prestigious Victorian family. Oliver's grandfather, the 4th Lord Lyttleton, was a close personal friend of Gladstone. Married to Gladstone's sister-in-law Mary Glynne, he had eight sons, including Sir Neville Lyttleton (Chief of General Staff) and Edward Lyttleton, Headmaster of Eton College. Of his four daughters, Lavinia – the second eldest, married Edward Talbot, later Bishop of Winchester. Their youngest son Lieutenant Gilbert Talbot, 7th Battalion The Rifle Brigade, was killed in action in the afternoon counter-attack at Zouave Wood, Hooge on 30 July 1915. Lieutenant Talbot, favourite cousin of Oliver, is buried at Sanctuary Wood Cemetery. Oliver's father, Alfred Lyttleton, was first married to Margot Tennant's sister Laura after whose premature death he married Edith Balfour, Oliver's mother.

11. Captain Jack Pixley was recommended for a Military Cross, but the recommendation was never confirmed.

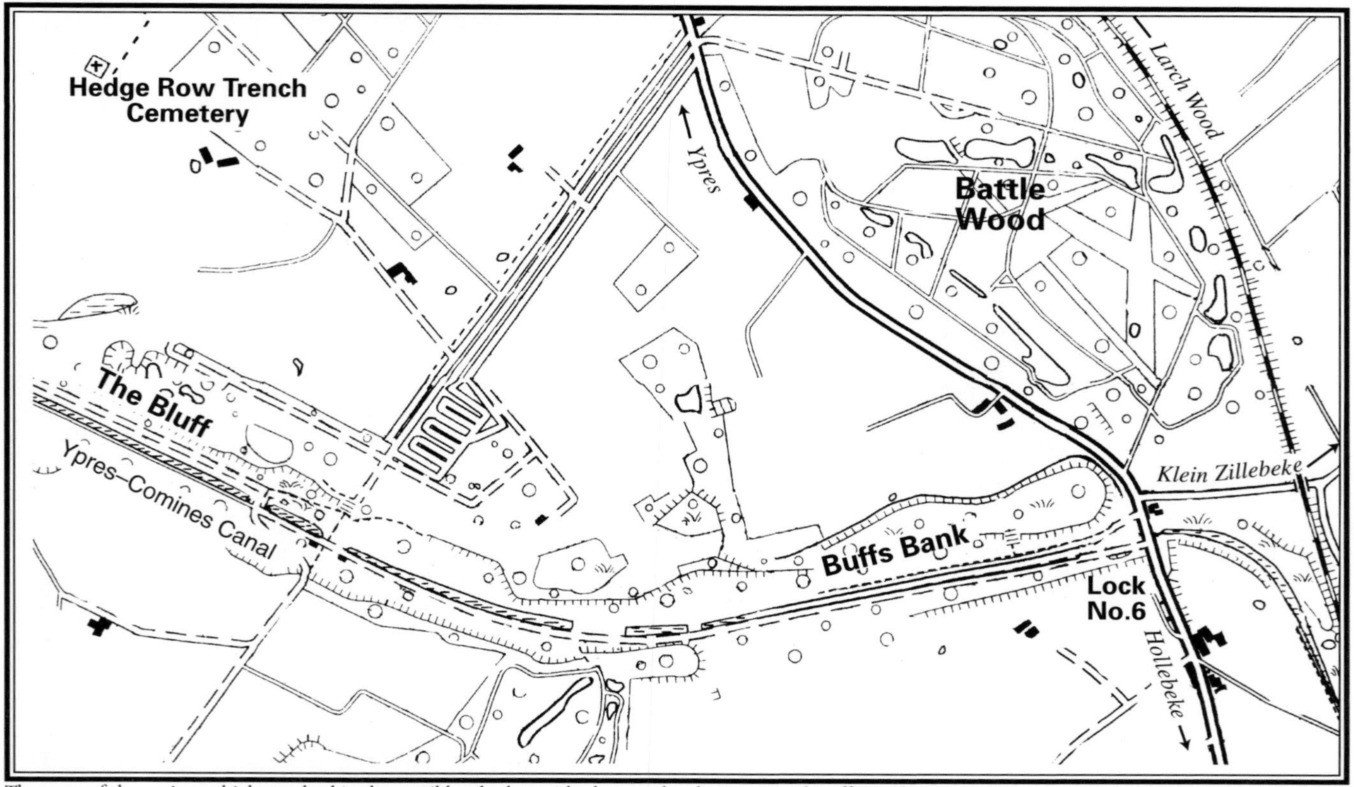

The area of the action which resulted in the spoil bank alongside the canal to be re-named Buffs Bank

Hedge Row Trench Cemetery

The Bluff

Ypres–Commes Canal

Ypres →

Battle Wood

Buffs Bank

Lock No.6

Hollebeke ←

Klein Zillebeke

Larch Wood

26

Whatever comes from the heart carries the heat and colour of its birthplace.
Oliver Wendell Holmes.

3

AN ARTIST AT WAR
Ernest Carlos 1883-1917
Spoil Bank, Ypres 1917

MEN FROM EVERY WALK of life, every strata of society, every class and trade served and fell on the Western Front during the Great War of 1914-18. Many of these hailed from the sporting and creative sphere of civilian life: sportsmen, poets, writers and artists are among those who fell victim and are included within this horrific loss of life. Their graves can be found in many of the hundreds of British cemeteries that mark the line of the old British front.

One such man was a thirty-year old artist from Bromley, Kent who, from his teenage years and through his brief military career until his death in 1917 during the Messines Offensive, built upon his growing reputation among the artistic fraternity.

Ernest Stafford Carlos was born into comfortable family circumstances in May 1883 at The Priory, Homesdale Road, Bromley, Kent to John Gregory Carlos and Anne Chessell Carlos. Not much is officially documented about his early education in and around Bromley, but there was no doubt that the vocation of an artist seemed to be the prevailing influence in his life. He had a canvas hung in the Royal Academy, London at the age of eighteen, plus a further thirteen works displayed there in various summer exhibitions, the latest of these being in 1915.

The outbreak of war in 1914 started eating away the best of the manpower of all the warring nations. with Carlos, thirty-years old at the time, watching the unfolding events from a distance, but the time came when the large casualty returns from France and Flanders and the severe manpower situation generally could no longer go unheeded and, during 1916 when the nation was reeling from the losses being reported from the various battles of the Somme, Carlos volunteered for military service and, like so many thousands of his countrymen, entered the war machine, .

27

After his initial training, he was considered suitable for a commission in the infantry, becoming a junior officer in the 8th Battalion, East Kent [The Buffs] Regiment, part of 17th Brigade, 24th Division, a reserve assault unit under the command of Major General L. J. Bols.

When Carlos joined them in early 1917, the division were in the Vimy Ridge area near Arras where they had been bystanders as the Canadian Corps attacked and captured the ridge in a snowstorm on 9 April 1917. He must have made many observations privately, being a spectator of this great battle where the dominion troops were superb, and one wonders what the artist within him thought of the military machine at work.

He was quite prolific during this period while off-duty, producing works with pen and brush. Like every young officer his overriding duty was to his men, but his drawings and paintings were abundant. Sketch books with many finely observed details of life at the front were left among his possessions after his death.

During the months of April-May 1917 the 24th Division received orders to move north to Flanders where General Plumer planned the 7 June Messines Offensive. The division left the Artois region to march northward in easy stages towards the battle area, south of Ypres.

The British had been planning the attack since 1916, the explosion of nineteen carefully laid mines being the opening to an offensive destined to secure the capture of the Messines Ridge, a height hitherto thought impregnable.

Marching north, Carlos used his spare time to capture on canvas that which took his imagination. Among the twenty pieces he completed during that trek to Flanders were: *Vimy Ridge, evening [21 April 1917]; On the Track of the Hun, on the march. Lieven near Lens, [April 1917]* (where the regiment had bivouacked); *Fires Burning at Ypres [June 1917]; French Farm Girl at Abeele, Poperinghe [1917]* and *Three Officers Playing Cards at Poperinghe [1917]*. These were typical of those he produced during that period. Perhaps lacking the sharp dramatics of battle, but typical of daily divisional life as seen by the artistic mind.

But battle and personal destiny loomed near as the battle arrangements were completed. The fighting divisions had reached the area just south of Poperinghe, west of Ypres, on 4 June. The day, 7 June 1917, for the opening of battle approached and his battalion was ordered to assemble near Zillebeke Lake the day before. This was to be the first major action for many of the men as it was for Ernest Carlos.

The results of the explosion of the nineteen mines brought a stunning success and the ridge passed into the hands of British and Empire troops for the first time since 1914. 7 June was a magnificent day for the much maligned British military and the enemy was thrown into early disarray before his usual resilience and counter-attacks restored the situation in parts. The fighting during the remainder of early June took on a grim stalemate.

During the early stage of the battle the 17th Brigade had been in divisional support near St. Eloi but ordered to advance to the Green Line near Oosttaverne Wood. On the 8th, the Buffs were ordered to retire to Triangular Dump south of Battle Wood for a short rest, relieving the 18th London [Irish] and 3rd Rifle Brigade. The Buffs battle headquarters was set-up in Larch Tree dug-outs.

The Buffs and remainder of the brigade were next in action on the 14 June, six days later Lieutenant Carlos was in their ranks as they attacked, the main objective, the line of a spoil bank – a thirty-foot high bank of spoil from the Comines Canal which ran close by. The bank was nearly 300 feet long and ran slightly south-west from the southern part of Battle Wood. Its extreme right hand position of the bank over-spilled into the end of the wood itself. It was the right hand sector of the bank the 17th Brigade would attack.

The enemy fought hard to hold this eminent landmark in their line, all of Battle Wood being of importance tactically, but the brigade were not to be denied. This bank of spoil saw infantry fighting of great intensity during 14 June before the 6th and 8th Buffs finally took it.[1] In their honour, the bank was named Buffs Bank.[2] Enemy counter-attacks were fierce and frequent, but were all beaten off. At 5.30 p.m the Germans called down a tremendous retaliatory fire on the defenders, lasting several hours, but the line held and at the end of the day the Buffs were still in control.

It is not known exactly when Ernest Carlos fell in this, his first major action. It could have been in the maelstrom of infantry fighting to secure the bank, or in the following artillery onslaught, but at the end of the day, he lay dead, an artistic talent extinguished in the hell of Flanders.

The position was held until early next day, 15 June, when The Buffs were finally relieved by the 2nd Battalion Leinster Regiment. The Buffs with the rest of the division retired to safe and clean reserve positions near Zillebeke where time would be allowed to regroup, take stock of their losses, clean equipment and receive new reinforcements to the battle-depleted units.

On this date, 17 June 1917, the Buffs found themselves at a reserve position at Burgomaster Farm near Zillebeke Lake, and an after-the-battle, roll call was taken. Taking into consideration the intensity of the battle, the overall casualty list for the action had not been as heavy as first feared. Although losing their commanding officer wounded during the day, three officers and fourteen other ranks were killed along with many others wounded. Major Vaughan stepped forward to take over the 8th Buffs as temporary commanding officer.

Lieutenant Carlos was listed as one of the officers killed on the bank during the period 14-15 June. After the fury of fighting moved away from the Battle Wood area, his body was found and given a decent burial at a place where most of the divisional dead had been laid to rest. A makeshift battlefield plot at Chester Farm had been set aside. This was near to Lock 5 on the canal at the extreme western point of Spoil Bank and here he rests to-day, a member of that great creative fraternity absorbed by the Great War[2]

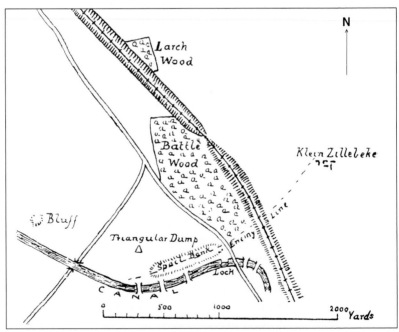

Buffs Bank from a sketch map in the Buffs regimental history. Note: 'Spoil Bank' is not the Spoil Bank shown on military maps. The 'officially' named bank is the one sited alongside the canal west of the Bluff and just south-west of Chester Farm.

Lieutenant Ernest S. Carlos
8th Battalion, The Buffs (East Kent Regiment)
Lieutenant Carlos is buried at Chester Farm Cemetery, Zillebeke. I. K. 36.

Notes

1. The approximate position of the Buffs' start line on 14th June prior to the attack would be abreast of Oak Dump British Cemetery to-day.

2. The eastern end of Buffs Bank is still evident in the undergrowth at Lock 6 Battle Wood.

3. The temporary burial plot at Chester Farm Zillebeke where Lieutenant Carlos can be found was enlarged after the Armistice to 414 British and Empire graves. There are also four German burials here.

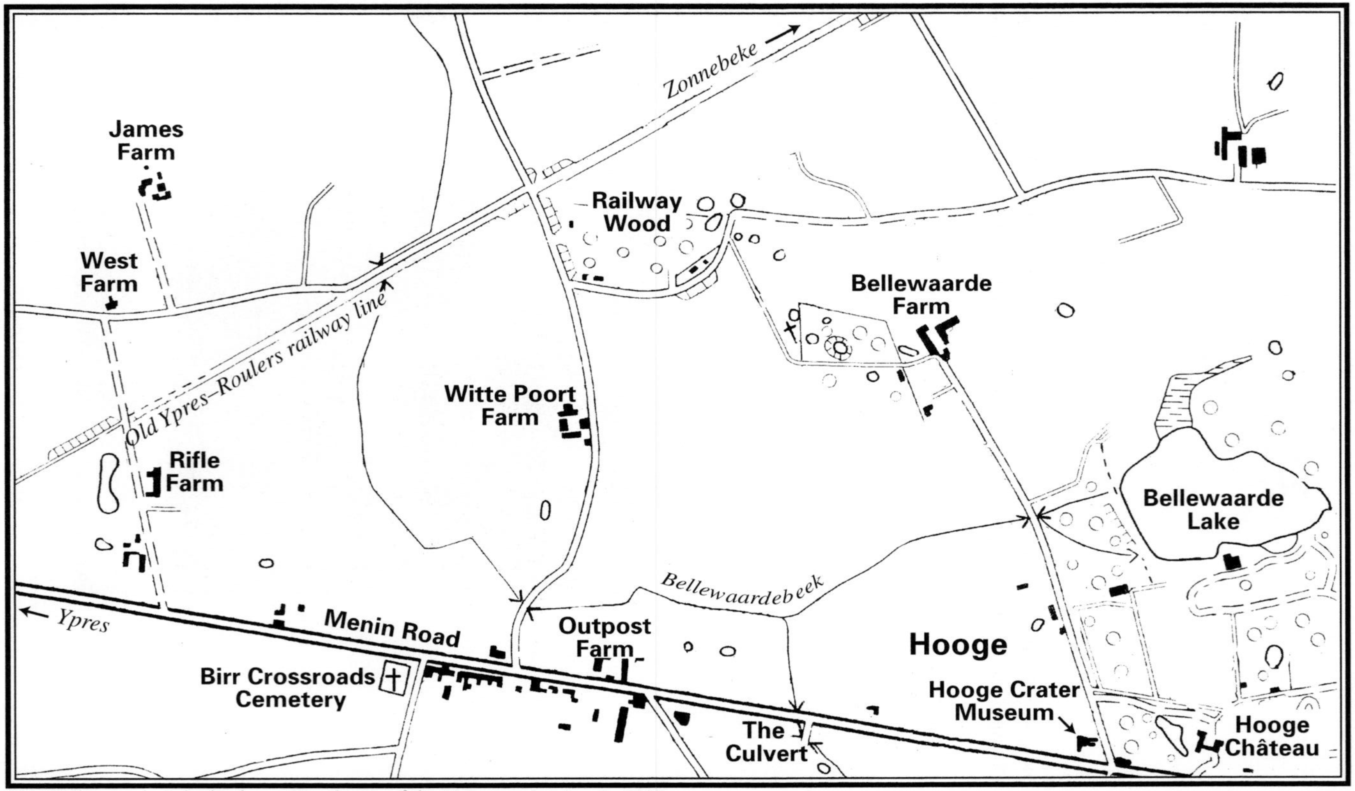
James Farm
West Farm
Zonnebeke
Railway Wood
Bellewaarde Farm
Old Ypres–Roulers railway line
Witte Poort Farm
Rifle Farm
Bellewaarde Lake
Bellewaardebeek
Ypres
Menin Road
Outpost Farm
Hooge
Birr Crossroads Cemetery
Hooge Crater Museum
The Culvert
Hooge Château
The Bellewaarde Lake/Railway Wood area of the Dragoons' action in 1915

'The boast of heraldry, the pomp of pow'r,
And all that beauty, all that wealth e'er gave,
Awaits alike th' inevitable hour,
The paths of glory lead but to the grave
Thomas Gray – Elegy Written in a Country Churchyard

4
INTO BATTLE – JULIAN OF THE 'ARD 'EAD
Captain Julian Henry Francis Grenfell, D.S.O.
1st (Royal) Dragoons, Ypres, 26 May 1915

O N 13 MAY, 1915, during the last few weeks of Second Ypres, an officer in the 1st (Royal) Dragoons was wounded near Hooge just two miles east of Ypres. The shard of shrapnel which pierced his skull seemed, initially, to be a wound of no undue significance, but within two weeks the young officer was dead, prompting widespread sorrow across the circles of English society where his family held a pivotal position in its upper echelons. The family's name was Desborough; the family seat Taplow Court in Buckinghamshire, and the officer, Captain, the Honourable Julian Henry Francis Grenfell D.S.O.

Born in 1818, in many ways Julian became the epitome of the British subaltern; With a classic upbringing and one of the Eton-and-Oxford set, he entered the British Army as was considered customary for the eldest son and heir of the aristocracy at this time. However, Julian was a most unusual child from a most unusual family and his mother's influence was to prove the dominant factor of his life. Ettie was the doyenne of an influential elite circle of Victorian high society known as *The Souls* whose members enthused and discoursed with wit and pseudo-intellectualism on philosophical and metaphysical concerns. The charming, attractive and sophisticated Ettie Desborough was at its core.[1]

With an ever-increasing patronage, the children of the families and their friends developed a more youthful and contemporary outlook and protagonists amongst them decided to establish a 'breakaway' group which they called *The Corrupt Coterie*.[2] Though Julian's mother had been the centre of *The Souls,* with *The Coterie* the emphasis of influence shifted to the Asquith children – especially Raymond, and away from the sphere of the Desborough domain.[3]

The Desborough family in 1910. From left to right – Billy aged 20, Monica aged 17 [the sister who was a VAD] Ettie, Imogan (sitting on Ettie's lap) Willy, Ivo aged 12 [the youngest brother] and Julian aged 22.

34

Julian was an altogether more complex individual than the hindsight of posterity has reflected, until recent years. Once thought of as the archetypal aristocrat and 'man of empire', a more careful inspection reveals that here was a young man of deeply disturbed sensibilities. On the one hand, eldest son and heir to one of the most socially attractive families in England, whilst on the other an independent thinker with a keen intellect who viewed his privilege and position with a good deal of disdain, feeling that his environment was rather superficial and that his ability to express any individuality within it was greatly inhibited. His mother's lifestyle and demeanour contributed greatly to this, her enthusiastic insistence and desire for the children to be permanently bright, sociable and successful led to the inclusion of an infamous phrase in one of his poems from his days at Eton, written clearly for the benefit of Ettie:

> To all the world I say "Hang it -
> I, who for 17 years of life
> Have trod this happy, bustling planet
> I won't go woman-hunting yet,
> I won't be made a social pet!

Another of Ettie's traits which caused Julian to suffer enormous resentment, jealousy and distaste was her penchant for the company of vibrant, young men. With many of her circle of admirers and lovers including Julian's friends and contemporaries, outbursts of anger and depression intensified throughout Julian's life, manifesting themselves in full-blown verbal battles between mother and son. As his days at Eton drew to a close his refusal to conform to the demands of Ettie's affected social conventions and values had established itself with Julian as 'fights for life'. Also, many of Julian's contemporaries had begun to question the sincerity and substance of the social fabric generated by *The Souls* which seemed to prompt even greater feelings of isolation within him.[4] At Eton he had continued to broaden his intellect and also excelled in sport, a trait inherited from his father. In addition, he had discovered a love of poetical expression through his forays into verse in which he showed considerable promise. However, to an extent, he continued the familiar theme of existing within a social framework within which he felt constrained and uncomfortable. Although editor of the official Eton College Chronicle, he was concurrently founder and editor of a rival sister paper called *The Outsider*, the content of which mocked the former more 'establishment' journal.[5]

In 1906 Balliol College, Oxford provided new scope for Julian to extend his abilities. He read classics and modern philosophy and was highly regarded by his Oxbridge contemporaries and tutors. His radical views however, were apparent in a book he wrote containing seven essays, the substance of which challenged and derided the conventions and lifestyle of his family:

> ... the world of etiquette, of manners, of social advancement, its atmosphere – the pungent atmosphere of afternoon tea.

The Ho. Julian Grenfell from a photograph taken at Taplow Court. The dog is the original of his poem entitled *The Black Greyhound*

During this period of intense melancholy he expressed a wish that 'social plans had one neck and me a knife'. He was increasingly regarded by many as cool and aloof and suffered a good deal from the mounting pressure by his mother to become more outgoing and involved in the constant rounds of social gatherings which were so torturous an ordeal for the young Julian.

After further bouts of depression, including time spent convalescing with his great-aunt Kate Cowper in Italy, Julian graduated from Balliol in 1910 and was subsequently offered a commission in the Royal Dragoon Guards. He was posted with the regiment to India and then on to South Africa although throughout his military service overseas he was still plagued by insecurities and a desire to find the happiness which always proved so elusive to him. One long-standing influence on Julian and his choice of career was the family friendship with Lord Kitchener. Tales of the South African campaign were recounted to Julian and his brother Billy "without the slightest swagger or self-praise" and had a considerable impact on the young aristocrat. Kitchener's modesty and dislike of state dinners and large occasions proved him a kindred spirit to Julian and this drew them together into a warm friendship, as reflected in their correspondence.[6] In 1914, after considering not for the first time a change of career, he decided that the summer would provide the ideal setting for commencing a new life venture involving one of his best friends from the Eton-and-Oxford set, Denys Finch-Hatton. Julian planned to join Denys and Jack Pixley in Nairobi at their 'Palatial residence' where many émigrés of the English elite were gathered. However, the outbreak of war intervened and his regiment was recalled to England and, arriving on 20 September 1914, went straight to Salisbury Plain, Wiltshire.

In many respects this turn of events provided an opportunity for Julian, to sweep away the old life with its stagnant, outmoded values, and prepare for the new with a strong sense that such universal catharsis would also purge the more personal demons of his own past: as Nicholas Mosley aptly surmised: "Life was a veil of tears and war a sponge to mop it up."

Julian's response to the outbreak of war reflects a consensus of patriotic feeling, so prevalent amongst his contemporaries:

Don't you think it has been a wonderful and almost incredible rally to the Empire? It reinforces one's failing belief in the Old Flag and the Mother Country and the Heavy Brigade and the Thin Red Line and all the Imperial Idea, which gets rather shadowy in peace time, don't you think?

After just over two weeks in England, Julian left for Flanders with his Regiment on the night of 5 October 1914.

In a letter of 3 November whilst positioned near Zandvoorde Julian relates an incident which is most revealing at a time when passions were running high with natural aggressive instincts towards the enemy uppermost in most of the regular serving soldiers:

We took a German Officer and some men prisoners in the wood the other day. One felt hatred for them as one thought of our dead; and as the Officer came by me, I scowled at him, and the men were cursing him. The Officer looked me in the face and saluted me as he passed, and I have never seen a man look so proud and resolute and smart and confident, in his hour of bitterness. It made me feel terribly ashamed of myself ...

As this war of movement continued, Julian's letters home began to convey a growing sense of underlying insecurities, thinly masked by a veil of confidence, most aptly surmised by his brother Billy as:

the mysticism and idealism, and that strange streak of melancholy which underlay Julian's war-whooping, sun-bathing, fearless exterior.

In a letter relating his experience of being under fire for the first time, Julian's natural sense of fear and caution is still apparent amidst an almost schoolboyish sense of revelry at the occasion:

I longed to be able to say that I like it, after all one has heard of being under fire for the first time. But it is beastly. I pretended to myself for a bit that I liked it, but it was no good ... After the firing had slackened, we advanced again a bit into the next group of houses, which were the edge of the village proper. I cannot tell you how muddling it is. We did not know which was our front. We did not know whether our own troops had come round us on the flanks, or whether they had stopped behind and were firing into us. And besides, a lot of German snipers were left in the houses we had come through, and every now and then bullets came singing by from God knows where. Four of us were talking and laughing in the road, when about a dozen bullets came with a whistle. We all dived for the nearest door, and fell over each other, yelling with laughter, into a very dirty outhouse ... Here we are, in the burning centre of it all, and I would not be anywhere else for a million pounds and the Queen of Sheba ...

Writing of the weapon which was to cause his mortal wound as an 'old friend', Julian, recalls a close encounter with a Jack Johnson with a good measure of light-hearted dismissal, accompanied once more by somewhat serious reflection:

You hear them coming for miles and everyone imitates the noise; then they burst with a plump and make a great hole in the ground, doing no damage unless they happen to fall into your trench or on to your hat. One landed within ten yards of me the other day, and only knocked me over and my horse. We both got up and looked at each other, and laughed. It did not even knock the cigarette out of my mouth .... About the shells; after a day of them, one's nerves are really absolutely beaten down. I can understand now why our infantry have to retreat sometimes; a sight which came as a shock to one at first, after being brought up in the belief that the English infantry cannot retreat ...

In mid-November Julian's battalion moved up into trenches north of Kleine Zillebeke in a wood close to the enemy trenches, in places only 40-50 yards away. It was whilst here, on 16 November, that he performed three single-handed patrols of German trenches in the space of 24 hours which won him a D.S.O. and promotion to Captain. This feat merits closer inspection for an insight into the considerable personal courage demanded to retrace dangerous ground after a single act of bravado. Julian relates in his own words:

I went out to the right of our lines, where the 10th were, and where the Germans were nearest. I took about 30 minutes to do 30 yards, then I saw the Hun trench, and I waited there a long time, but could see or hear nothing. It was about 10 yards from me. Then I heard some Germans talking and saw one put his head up over some bushes about 10 yards behind the trench. I could not get a shot at him, I was too low down, and of course I could not get up. So I crawled on again very slowly to the parapet of their trench. It was very exciting. I was not sure that there might have been someone there, or a little further along the trench. I peered through their loophole and saw nobody in the trench. Then the German behind put his head up again. He was laughing and talking. I saw his teeth glistening against my fore-sight, and I pulled the trigger very slowly. He just grunted, and crumpled up. The others got up and whispered to each other. I do not know which were most frightened, them or me. I think there were four or five of them. They could not trace the shot, I was flat behind their parapet and hidden. I just had the nerve not to move a muscle and stay there. My heart was fairly hammering. They did not come forward, and I could not see them, as they were behind some bushes and trees, so I crept back inch by inch.

In the afternoon he returned to the same section of trench but saw nobody. After waiting for an hour there, some 60 yards out in No Man's Land, he came back to report the trench empty. The following morning however, just before dawn, Julian had again crawled out to the same spot and explains:

... a single German came through the woods towards the trench. I saw him 50 yards off. He was coming along upright and careless, making a great noise. I heard him before I saw him. I let him get within 25 yards, and shot him in the heart. He never made a sound. Nothing for 10 minutes, and then there was a noise and talking, and a lot of them came along, through the wood behind the trench about 40 yards from me. I counted about 20, and there were more coming. They halted in front, and I picked out the one I thought was the officer, or sergeant. He stood facing the other way, and I had a steady shot at him behind the shoulders. He went down and that was all I saw. I went back at a sort of galloping crawl to our lines ...

On his return he warned of an enemy movement and, half an hour later when the Germans attacked, the waiting troops were prepared and the enemy was swiftly dealt with.

He had declined a staff job as ADC to General Pulteney, considering it to be too 'cushy' an option and he was reluctant to relinquish his new-found status as a valued and admired fighting soldier. After returning home for a week's leave late in December Julian returned to the battalion now in the Salient and a month later was moved to trenches slightly north of Kleine Zillebeke. In a letter home he writes typically up-beat news for his family's consumption:

I was asleep, when suddenly there was a deafening crash, and half of the dug-out roof fell on to my face. I ran out and found old Sammy being pulled out by the legs from under the ruin of his dug-out, amid yells of laughter ...

Julian's private diary however, reveals an altogether more genuine and uncensored account of the same incident:

... I heard noise of bomb dropping on top of dug-out. Petrified. Lost self-control – lay still, clenching my hands for twenty seconds ...

A letter written to the attractive Virginian living next door to Taplow Court – Nancy Astor, further exemplifies the widening gulf between Julian's rather blasé exterior and his truer private feelings about the war:

Nancy, you can't think of the soul in this war. It is absolutely at a discount. It is much better for us to leave it out altogether, if one can – and all sentiment too.[7]

In March the battalion went into billets at Blaringhem. It was here that Julian wrote a somewhat sardonic poem dedicated to 'those on the staff'. Then, the following month, Julien decided to spend a forty-eight leave on a visit to Paris. The short trip had an extraordinay impact on the young man who indulged in various pleasures, describing the visit as 'the biggest experience of New Things I've ever had in my life'.

On 21 April, Julian's sister Monica – a V.A.D. at Wimereaux near Boulonge – was surprised to receive an impromptu visit from her brother who had accordingly taken a considerable detour on his return to the front. Having only recently enquired of some of her new patients as to the whereabouts of the Royals (The Dragoons) she describes her disbelief at hearing of her brother's arrival at the hospital:

> One day, when I was upstairs collecting equipment for the patients, the charming ill-looking nurse rushed up to me calling: "Grenfell, Grenfell, your brother is here." I could not believe it, having thought there was no chance of any leave at this time. So she went on: "He's here, he's come to see you; and I wanted to tell you!"

Although seemingly "to good to be true", brother and sister seized the opportunity to enjoy an hour and a half together, talking to Monica's patients in the ward before walking in the sunshine to have tea in Wimereaux where Monica saw him on to his train at the station, to return to the battalion.[8]

Julian arrived back in the Salient as Second Ypres began where he was billeted at Thiennes and then at Houtkerque, near Watou. On 29 April Julian recorded in his diary that he had written what was to become one of the most well-known poems of the war, synonymous with the sentiments of its early stages. He drew richly on his familiarity with, and appreciation of, the classics and the poem is unquestionably one of the finest singular works to emerge from the war. Julian's entry in his diary for that day reads:

> Moved off 8 a.m. towards Pop. Brigade rested in field. Rested all day, and got back to our farm at 7.30 p.m. Pork chops for dinner. Wonderful sunny lazy days – but longing to be up and doing something. Slept out. Wrote poem – 'Into Battle'.

On 9 May the battalion moved to wooden huts at Vlamertinghe a little way up the Brielen Road. Julian's diary mentions walking through the outskirts of Ypres:

> ... blazing in summer night; stink, rotting horses and men. Drew rations on road and got into trench 11.30 p.m. Detachments of Argyll and Sutherlands and Royal Fusiliers, dead beat, in our trench.

By 12 May the battalion was in the second line of trenches between Bellewaarde Lake and The Ypres–Roulers railway line half-a-mile to the north. In the early hours of the following morning the Germans began a heavy bombardment on the 'little hill of death' and Julian, acting as observer (described by General Pulteney as strolling around 'as if he were on a river') was knocked over by the blast of a shell which tore his coat. Returning to the observation post with the news that the enemy were outflanking their positions, he volunteered to take a message through to the Somerset Yeomanry in the trenches in front of his position. A Company Commander remembered Julian walking up to him, coolly introducing himself whilst under heavy fire, then pointing out: "You once gave me a mount with the Belvoir Hounds.". Returning from these positions with further messages he was accompanying the Brigade General back up toward the railway line when a shell landed close to both men with a small stray fragment entering Julian's skull.

Back at the casualty clearing station, he wrote to Ettie explaining:

> ... I stopped a Jack Johnson with my head, and my skull is slightly cracked. But I am getting on splendidly.

The letter was signed 'Julian of the 'ard 'ead.'

From here he was deemed well enough to be sent back to Base Hospital at Boulogne though his journey, described by him as 'terrible' can hardly have improved his chances of surviving his head wound. At the hospital where a close family friend was also recovering, Julian's response to the surgeon who asked him how long he had been unconscious after being hit was typical of his humour.[9] Drawing on his boxing experience he replied: "I was up before the count".

On Julian's arrival at hospital, Monica had sent a telegram home to say that Julien would soon be back in England and therefore to cancel plans to embark for Boulogne. However, the following day, 16 May, Julian was X-rayed and the wound was discovered to be far more serious than had been supposed. The shell-splinter had entered the skull to a depth of one-and-a-half inches and there was damage to the brain. An operation would be essential, followed by a critical ten days. Monica therefore sent another telegram telling the parents to sail for France as originally planned and with permission immediately granted from the Admiralty, Ettie and Willy Desborough crossed the Channel that night on an ammunition supply ship.

Three days later, on 20 May, Billy, newly arrived with his Rifle Brigade battalion, was granted a day's leave to visit Julian before being despatched to the front.[10] Julian's cheerful demeanour obscured much of the gravity of his condition and for a time everyone felt that he appeared to show considerable signs of stability and improvement.

Although the family continued their vigil at Julian's bedside, his condition deteriorated until finally, on 26 May, he died. Even with the death of her son, Ettie's account of his final hours reveals her romantic obsession with the beauty of death which had been so typical of the Soul's thinking: "A shaft of sunlight came in at the darkened window and fell across his feet".

No mourning colours were permitted at his funeral which Ettie designed as a ceremony of 'purification' to reflect the nobility and sanctity of a heroic death in the tradition of the epic Greek tragedies, as wild flowers and oak leaves were laid over his grave, which today lies within the confines of Boulogne Eastern Military Cemetery. Only in death had Julian provided perhaps his first and only truly complete gesture of conciliation to his mother's world.

Tributes poured in from far and wide; the family were inundated with consolatory messages, many of which were from those who themselves would find soldier's graves before the war's conclusion.

One of the most poignant of these tributes was that of his brother Billy who, within just two short months would himself be a victim of the fighting in Flanders, being killed barely a mile from where Julian had been hit. In October 1910, when Julian had left for India with his regiment Billy, writing to his mother from Oxford where Julian had spent a last weekend with him saying his goodbyes, encapsulated sentiments that would bear uncanny relevance to the manner of Julian's lingering death over four years later:

I don't think people ought ever to be allowed to say goodbye; they ought just to fade away silently without these soul-harrowing seconds, and to leave one to put the past in a frame of gold.

In a memoir recalling his days as a schoolmaster at Eton, Hugh Macnaghten provides a fitting 'frame of gold' as he recalls his final encounter with the young cavalry officer:

It was the first morning of the Easter holidays, 1904, and 'Savage was I sitting' at my desk, writing reports, rather wearily. Suddenly in the passage outside there was the sound of a horse's hoofs, and then a boy bending from his saddle looked in at the window and said, "I have brought my new horse to show you".

Rider and horse were as glorious as the riders and horses from the Parthenon frieze who for nearly fifteen years have made the entrance to that passage beautiful. "Once more the heavenly Power makes all things new," I thought to myself as I looked at the boy, with the dew of April morning on his face, glorying in the horse he rode... It was Julian Grenfell. The memory of his coming from Taplow Court to show me his new horse abides unforgettable. Years afterwards I met the two brothers for the last time as they were riding home through Dorney village. When Julian died, after writing "Into Battle" a glory passed from the earth.

> With infinite desire
> You thrilled, the lover's way -
> Your dreams were fire.
>
> You loved the stars, the sun,
> Brave games and noble books,
> And graced each triumph won
> With golden looks,
>
> Till last and best the war
> Brought joy at every breath,
> And life became a star
> Undimmed by death.

Perhaps however, the most eloquent and enduring tribute to Julian is that written by his own hand in the final verse of *Into Battle*, a work which has assured his claim to immortality – exceeding all that his mother could have hoped for – and which has enhanced our increasing respect and admiration for a man whose talents and abilities were never truly appreciated in his own lifetime.

> The thundering line of battle stands,
> And in the air death moans and sings,
> But day shall clasp him with strong hands,
> And night shall fold him in soft wings."

Captain Julian Henry Francis Grenfell, D.S.O.
1st (Royal) Dragoons
Captain Grenfell is buried in Boulogne Eastern Cemetery, Pas de Calais, France. II. A. 18

Notes:

1. Members of *The Souls* were: Willy and Ettie Desborough, Arthur Balfour, George Curzon, George Wyndham, Evan Charteris, Margot Tennant (later Asquith), Hugh & Mary Elcho, Tommy and Charty Ribblesdale. Peter Parker, in his study of *The Great War and Public School Ethos* describes them as – 'a group of lugubrious, narcissistic and highly influential aristocrats, who spent much time descanting on the beauty of death. Any decrease in their circle was greeted with a chorus of rapturous keening. Death beds were rushed to as eagerly as balls; gazing upon expiring members of the circle reassured the survivors of the beauty and radiance of death.'

In 1894 Herbert Asquith married Margot, one of Sir Charles Tennant's daughters, whose sister Charlotte (Charty) married Tommy Lister (Lord Ribblesdale). Their son, Lieutenant, the Honourable Charles Alfred Lister 1st County of London Yeomanry, died on 26th August 1915 when a wound caused by a shell fragment turned gangrenous. He is buried in East Mudros Military Cemetery, Lemnos. Margot's eldest brother Edward (1st Lord Glenconner) married Pamela Wyndham. Their son, Lieutenant the Honourable Edward Wyndham Tennant 4th Grenadiers was killed in action on the Somme in 1916. Edward, known as 'Bimbo' or 'Bim', was a friend and fellow 4th officer of Harold Macmillan (later attached to the 2nd in April 1916 after being wounded in action at the Battle of Loos). One of Herbert's three sons – Herbert (Beb) married Cynthia Charteris daughter of Hugh and Mary Elcho and sister of Hugo (Ego) and Ivo Charteris both killed in action. Second Lieutenant, the Honourable Ivo Alan Charteris 1st Grenadiers was killed in action on 17 October 1915, and is buried in Sailly-Labourse Communal Cemetery, France. Captain, Lord Hugh Francis Charteris Elcho, Royal Gloucestershire Hussars was mistakenly reported as taken prisoner at Damascus but had in fact been killed at Katia on 23 April 1916. His name is on the Jerusalem Memorial, Israel.

2. Diana Manners describes *The Coterie's* pride as 'unshocked by words, unshocked by drink and unashamed of decadence and gambling – Unlike-Other-People, I'm afraid'. Of the nucleus of young men in the Coterie most were destined to find premature graves in military cemeteries across the battlegrounds of Europe.

3. Raymond Asquith was one of the brightest stars of his generation and the fulcrum of *The Coterie.* In 1907 he married Katharine Horner, daughter of Frances and John Horner of Mells Park, Somerset. Lieutenant Asquith 3rd Grenadiers died from a bullet wound received during the Battle of the Somme on 15 September 1916, and is buried in Guillemont Road Cemetery. His original grave marker hangs on the wall of the Horner Chapel in the village church at Mells. Katharine's brother Lieutenant Edward William Horner 18th Hussars, died of wounds from a German sniper on 21 November 1917. He is buried at Rocquigny-Equancourt Road British Cemetery, Manancourt, near Cambrai. Katharine's mother was a close friend of Lady Manners {known to all as Con} who became a close friend and confidante of Raymond. Con's son John Manners was killed in action in 1914. Con's daughter Betty married Raymond's brother Herbert {Oc}. Con's niece Diana Manners was one of three alluring sisters who became an integral part of the Coterie. Julian fell hopelessly in love with Marjorie but she married the Marquis of Anglesey. The other sister Violet {Letty} married the eldest of the Charteris brothers Hugo {Ego}. The sisters' permissive and somewhat bohemian demeanour earned them the disapproval of Julian's mother who called them, somewhat scathingly, the Hotbed.

4. Raymond relates the experience of one of his closest friends – Auberon {Bron} Herbert's sojourn at Taplow Court in 1906 – 'He has been living with the Grenfells in the full flow of the social tide these last two months and now he creeps in and out of their house by the back door and is conducted straight to his bedroom by a servant holding a green umbrella before him to prevent his seeing or being seen. I think I am coming round to his view. There are half a dozen women and perhaps a dozen men whose company I enjoy – but not in the way one gets it in London, tempered by a hundred conventions and restrictions and pomposities with bows and grimaces and hurry and clatter and insincerity – women twittering like tired birds and men tinkling like empty glasses." Captain, Lord Auberon {Bron} Thomas Lucas attached R.F.C. was shot down over enemy lines on 3 November 1916, during the Battle of the Somme and is buried at H.A.C. Cemetery, Ecoust-St Mein.

5. The editorial team of *The Outsider* with Julian at Eton in 1906 included Pat Shaw-Stewart, Robin Laffin, Edward Horner, Charles Lister, Cecil Gold and Ronald Knox. Cecil Gold became Lieutenant and Adjutant in the 5th Royal Berks and was killed on the Ovillers-Albert road on 3 July 1916, in the Battle of the Somme. He is buried in Aveluy Communal Cemetery Extension. Ronald Knox – celebrated intellectual, old Etonian and Balliol man was a friend and associate of a great many of the extended Coterie – is buried in the churchyard at Mells next to the manor house inhabited by the Horner family. Another burial here is Siegfried Sassoon, initiated into the Catholic faith in 1957 by Monsignor Knox by virtue of his friendship with Katherine Asquith (née Horner) who had embraced the Catholic faith in 1924.

6. Julian was also Kitchener's page at the delayed coronation of King Edward in

August 1902. Julian had first met Kitchener 3 years earlier at Taplow Court, whilst home for the holidays from Eton. He wrote of their meeting: "He asked me to come for a walk, and we went for over an hour. He found out that I was to be a soldier, and asked me what regiment I was going in for, and how I was getting on at school, and a great many other questions; he told me a great many things about the army, and yet he never mentioned himself at all, and I had not the least idea who he was."

7. Nancy Astor, wife of Lord Waldorf Astor, became the first woman to take her seat in the Houses of Parliament. For many years the Desboroughs and the Astors were estranged neighbours, largely due to Ettie's dislike of the dazzling and independent American beauty. However, in spite of this, Nancy became a close friend and confidante of not only Julian, but more especially his younger brother Billy.

8. In her book *Bright Armour: Memories of Four Years of War* Monica describes a conversation with Julian whilst waiting on the station platform for his train. Julian asked what she thought of the poem *Into Battle* and she replied that, although she had been told it was brautiful, she had not seen it herself. She also recalls that a copy arrived in the post for her the following day. If this conversation did take place at the time, then it occured on 21 April, eight day's before the entry dated in Julian's diary and the generally accepted date of the poem's creation. It may therefore be entirely possible that earlier drafts of the poem existed, dating from a slightly earlier period, and that they were sent to the members of the family for their consumption before being finalised into the ultimate draft as known to posterity on 29 April.

9. Receiving treatment in the hospital at the same time was Edward Horner of whom Sir John French had personally telegrammed Haldane: "Horner suffering from penetrating abdominal wound, serious nature – doing well as can be expected." The Horners received similar permission to the Desboroughs to cross to France, happening to meet Diana Manners at Boulogne station on their way to visit their son. Diana wrote to Shaw-Stewart on the chance encounter, adding that: "Edward had been hit by a shrapnel bullet which had been found nestling in his clothes" and which had gone through one kidney which was later removed.

11. Billy was granted a further day's leave on 29 May, the day after Julian's burial. He spent the afternoon with his parents and sister Monica in Boulogne before leaving for the front. They never saw him again.

Second Lieutenant, the Honourable Gerald William Grenfell {Billy}, 8th Rifle Brigade was killed in action in the fighting at Hooge on 30 July 1915. Also in this battalion were Second Lieutenants Sidney Woodroffe V.C. and Keith Rae.

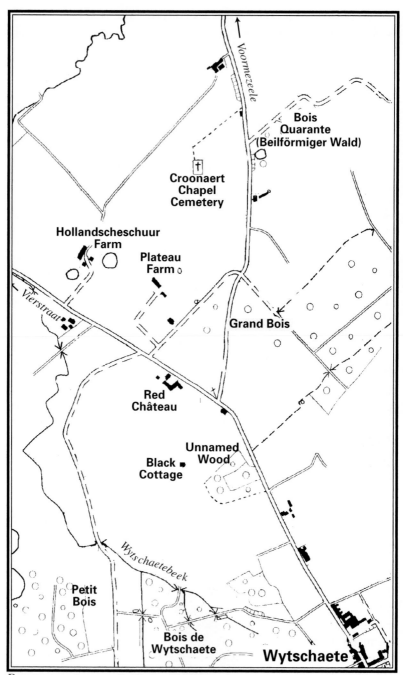

Bois Quarante, known as Beilfömiger Wald by the Germans, scene of one of Hitler's actions

And thereby hangs a tale.
Shakespeare – The Taming of the Shrew.

5

ADOLF HITLER AT YPRES
16th Bavarian Reserve Infantry Regiment
Bois Quarante, November 1914

D URING THE GREAT WAR of 1914 to 1918, powerful men manipulated, moved, planned and manoeuvred vast armies, caring not for the exalted or the lowest ranking soldier serving on either side of the line. Many of the rank and file were to be influenced by their experiences during this conflict, carrying those experiences with them through the twenties and thirties to the outbreak of another conflict between the same adversaries. Many men of high profile, Churchill, Eden, Alexander, Macmillan to name just a few of the well known personalities, were so influenced. But these were men of rank. Rarely does the foot-soldier take the opportunity to exploit his

Adolf Hitler in 1914

experience and make a name for himself. One such was a certain Adolphus Hitler, better known to the world as Adolf Hitler.

In 1914, 25-years old and with burning patriotism and high enthusiasm, he was serving in the first winter of the war as an infantry runner with the 16th Bavarian Reserve Infantry Regiment, amongst men recruited and drawn generally from the Munich area. The 16th Regiment was then part of the 12th Brigade serving in the 6th Bavarian Reserve Division of the Imperial German Army. There is no doubt, that his experiences in the front line during the war, and the fate of the German Army in 1918 deepened his sense of patriotism, affected him greatly throughout the thirties and conditioned much of his thinking in the volatile post-war period.

He was certainly destined to be a prime mover in the thinking of the German peoples, and the course of events which would take place and those terrible years of the early forties, affecting all the peoples of Europe, was certainly rooted in his early upbringing and tempered. in the war years, Much of what we have become today has its origins with this Austrian of common birth, born in April 1889 at Braunau, a tiny hamlet near Linz in Austria.

His service in actions from Flanders in the north to Cambrai in the south had not left him untouched. Narrowly escaping death on several occasions, he had been badly wounded in the hip, which needed a spell in hospital, badly gassed in the final stages of the war, and recommended for and awarded two Iron Crosses, First and Second class, during the years of conflict. The period left him with an angry sense of grievance and injustice, especially with the harsh terms of the Peace Treaty of Versailles of 1919 under which his beloved Fatherland would be shamed and caused to suffer considerably.

His country had been laid low by betrayal on the home front, by political influences, and out-of-control economic forces. This would stay with him for years as he chose to become politically active, as well as vengeful in thought and spirit. Like many serving soldiers, it had sorely affected him when Field Marshal Ludendorf contacted the Allies in the autumn of 1918 to seek terms for an Armistice after German High Command had conceded failure at the River Marne. Hitler himself, like thousands of his compatriots, had never doubted a final and glorious German victory.

From all accounts, he was popular with his fellow soldiers, due to his being reliable in a crisis, a characteristic he constantly demonstrated. He could always be depended upon to help a sick or wounded comrade and his zeal to serve his country both in war, and in later years was infectious.[1] He never tired of informing his friends that in the sureness of time, his day would come, and they would remember him. How many of those who served alongside Adolf Hitler and survived the battles of the 16th Bavarian Reserve Infantry Regiment, would recall those words twenty years or so hence?

There is no doubt that whatever great events of state were to overtake Hitler and Germany in the decades that followed the Great War, he would always find time to discuss his service days on the front line, particularly in Flanders during the final months of 1914. This was where he first tasted the heady atmosphere of combat, and this experience was etched deep within him.

He would talk enthusiastically with anyone who had shared the same dramatic moments, and at the time of the Munich Crisis of 1938 was most interested to know that Anthony Eden, later the Earl of Avon and Prime Minister of England, then part of the British negotiating team, had in fact served for a period in 1915 at Ploegsteert Wood, south of Messines in Belgium, with the 21st King's Royal Rifle Corps. Although Hitler had never actually served in the wood, he would have been aware of the woodland mass on a daily basis when the 16th Bavarians had their regimental headquarters at Betlheem Farm on the slopes of the Messines Ridge just north of the wood in the Autumn months of 1914. His post of duty at this time was as a regimental runner, and despatch messenger housed safely in the vaults of Messines Church perched safely on top of the ridge.

It is a tantalising thought to think of Winston Churchill, that other great powerhouse of the Second World War who also had a shared experience of this sector albeit in early 1916 as a surprisingly efficient Commander of the 6th Battalion Royal Scots Fusiliers, 9th (Scottish) Division. If these two goliaths had maybe met across the negotiating table in 1939-40, a personal discussion of politics mixed with memories of those shared heady experiences in Flanders during the Great War might have prevented later events. Sadly, at that critical period of negotiation, Winston Churchill was in no position to participate at such a level, so the option is a debatable one only.

That the Flanders of 1914 was prominent in the memory of this 25-year old former private soldier there is no doubt and none of it more so than an insignificant piece of woodland, Bois Quarante, perched perilously on the western tip of the mighty Messines Ridge, and tucked in alongside Grand Bois at the village of Wytschaete.

With the British Army itself engaged in a titanic struggle around the historic little town of Ypres at this time, holding off the advancing divisions of the Kaiser, this piece of the front was a responsibility of the French, but the fighting hereabouts was no less bloodthirsty.

Bois Quarante known as Axe or Hatchet Wood to the British, and indicated on German sketch maps of the time as Beilförmiger Wald, would be the first place that the name of Hitler would find its way into the minds of the German Military and regimental records.[2] There, he would again pose his steadfastness in battle in a most able way, and be instrumental in helping to save the life of a grateful regimental commander Lieutenant-Colonel Englehardt.

The little wood near Wytschaete would be etched in the conscience of Hitler for the rest of his days, demonstrated in 1940 after the fall of France when the first thing on his agenda was to revisit Flanders and the places so familiar to him in 1914.

He would recall that on a critical day in the balance of the First Battle of Ypres on Halloween Day, 31 October 1914, a day when the British were mounting valuable actions all along their line at Ypres to avert a crisis, the 16th Bavarians had been actively engaged around the village of Gheluvelt on its prominent ridge, abreast the Menin Road, east of Ypres.

The fighting had been heavy, and Hitler had played his part, so much so that his conduct under fire when the Regiment had lost two commanders did not escape notice. His reliability was rewarded by promotion to the post of regimental despatch runner, which would undoubtedly have pleased him.

The line held around Ypres; the stubborn British were in no mood to give way, and the battle began to subside around Gheluvelt after a period of fierce action which stretched from 20 October until 1 November 1914. It all added up to infuriating failure for the massed German infantry waiting to smash through to the little town, get to the

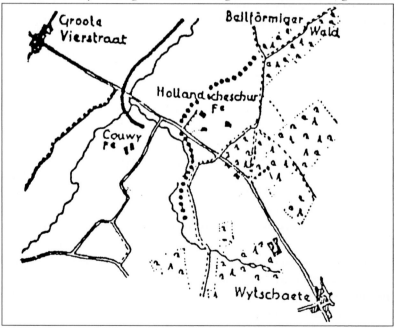

Beilförmiger Wald shown on a map in the 16th Bavarian Reserve Infantry Regiment History

coast and delight their waiting Kaiser at nearby Menin. It was not to be.

The selection of Hitler to the arduous post of a regimental runner would soon bring him further to the notice of the authorities.

The 6th Bavarian Reserve Division, of which the 16th Regiment was a part, now moved west in early November to the Wytschaete front, just as the British sector began to quieten down. The French, held the little wood of Beilförmiger Wald and resisted all German attempts to advance across the intervening space between the wood and Grand Bois. The French defensive fire was unrelenting.

The Regimental records show two more attempts would be made on 15 and 16 of November. Twice the confident Germany infantry would advance across the open ground that separated the two woods.

The first attempt on 15 November by the 16th Regiment was hardly any more successful than the previous ones, and infantry losses were mounting as the accurate French fire from the tree-line mounted a curtain of flying lead that the Germans found difficult to penetrate.

Their command was adamant that Beilförmiger Wald would be captured no matter what the cost, and a second attempt was mounted in the morning of the 16 November. This time, the relentless pressure paid off, and it would be here that a defining moment occurred in Hitler's own personal story. It was here in front of the little wood rippling with French fire and German artillery explosions that Adolf Hitler would distinguish himself before his superiors and warrant a recommendation for bravery.

As the fire intensified, Adolf Hitler felt his tunic ripped by a small piece of shrapnel. A close shave and one of several he would experience in the war (further proof to him that these near brushes with death demonstrated destiny had him marked out for greatness). Then he noticed Lieutenant-Colonel Englehardt walking bravely up the bullet-swept road parallel with the attack to encourage and support his men as they neared the objective. Near a small wayside shrine which was burning fiercely on the left hand side of the road, Englehardt was spotted by French defenders who began to turn their fire upon him. He seemed oblivious to the danger, and it would prove suicidal not to take some evasive action. Hitler spotted the danger to his commanding officer, and oblivious to any personal danger, he leapt on to the road and into the maelstrom of fire, and with the assistance of another orderly, Private Bachman, protected the Colonel, and quickly hustled him into the protective safety of a wayside ditch that ran the length of the road, until the immediate danger was over.

This second determined attempt by the Bavarians to capture the wood was successful and the brave French defenders were finally ousted from the wood which remained in German hands until the British 19th Butterfly Division captured it during the Messines offensive in June 1917.

Lieutenant-Colonel Englehardt made a note of the initiative and bravery shown by this quiet reflective soldier from Munich, and mentally made provision to recommend him for a bravery reward. It was his intention so to do, but a couple of days later as his list of awards was being drawn up, his headquarters was rocked by a direct hit from a shell, killing several therein and seriously wounding Englehardt himself, bringing his war to a conclusion. His loss to the men of the regiment was a severe blow to their morale as he was a highly respected and very popular officer. Hitler himself, who had been in the headquarters shortly before the shell caused the damage, had been ordered to leave on an errand and, from this stroke of luck, drew the conclusion that his 'miraculous' escape, one of a sequence of escapes he would experience in the war years, was an indication that he was destined for greater things.

The list of awards for the November action at Beilförmiger Wald went ahead, and although expecting more, (an Iron Cross First Class maybe), Hitler was still delighted to write home to friends on 2 December 1914, that he had received the Iron Cross Second Class due to the fact that he was a staff member at the time of his action. It was still a crowning moment in his soldier's life at that time, and one he would recall proudly to one and all.

Following the end of 1914 and the Ypres battles, Hitler played his part fully in all the campaigns in which the Bavarians were engaged: Loos in 1915; Fromelles and on the Somme in 1916; Arras, and Flanders again in 1917. It was at the village of Ligny Thilloy (Somme) in October 1916 near his regimental headquarters, that he was severely wounded in the hip which needed hospitalisation and a period of recovery at home in Germany. After being pronounced fit again, and after much lobbying, he got himself sent back to his beloved regiment, the 16th Bavarians.

In August 1918 at the Marne when the Germans were almost at the gates of Paris itself, he personally captured four French prisoners, and was beside himself with joy, to at last receive the coveted Iron Cross

First Class.[1] This was a culmination of what he had fought for all along. An apex of hope and ambition.

Temporarily blinded by gas at Wervik in Flanders which laid him low in October 1918, his war too, finally came to an angry conclusion as the hospital train with its full complement of pain and sorrow lumbered back towards a defeated Germany, allowing him plenty of time to ruminate, and begin to give vent to his paranoiac hatred of the Marxism he could see engulfing his beloved homeland and, likewise to world Jewry against whom he would wreak a terrible revenge.

His adventures in Flanders were only the beginning!

Notes:

1. Reports and opinions on Adolph Hitler tend to be controversial. A short article on him in *New Statesman*, 29 July 1933 reads: " ... when a man named Franz Xavier Huber, a veteran who had had a leg shot away before Verdun in 1917, told me stories of a curious fellow who had been in his regiment at the front . . . .

The thing that had struck him most about "Private Hitler" was his grandiloquence. He was neither popular nor the reverse with his fellows; they just smiled at him and his vague rambling speeches on everything in the world and out of it. He acquired very swiftly the reputation of being what in the British Army is called "an old soldier." That is, he showed distinct talent in voiding disagreeable tasks, but he knew on which side his bread was buttered. He interested himself particularly in the important question of seeing the officers' washing was done or doing it himself. This secured for him the good graces of the colonel who removed him from the more constant dangers of the trenches and appointed him runner between regimental head-quarters and the front line.

Though he got the Iron Cross of the second class, no one in the regiment ever looked upon Hitler as any sort of hero; indeed they rather admired him for the skill with which he avoided hot corners. The regimental records contain not a line concerning an award of the Iron Cross of the first class to Hitler, though in latter years he has taken to wearing it prominrently in his self-constructed uniform."

2) In the early 1970s when the then owner of the Bois Quarante, the late Andre Bequart was establishing the wood as a museum, he spoke often of the day in June 1940 after the fall of France when Hitler came to visit him and his father, recounting with enthusiasm his service and battle experience in the area, identifying the exact spot where he won his Iron Cross with the Lieutenant-Colonel Englehardt incident.

If Andre Bequart had lived and his plans come to fruition, the wood had the potential to become a major attraction on the Western Front with its pill-boxes, trench systems, mine-shafts, and mountains of shell cases and battlefield artifacts.

With his death in the early 1990's, the wood fell neglected. Its further development as a museum, currently under investigation, should see it blossom again as a place for battlefield visitors to go to in the near future.

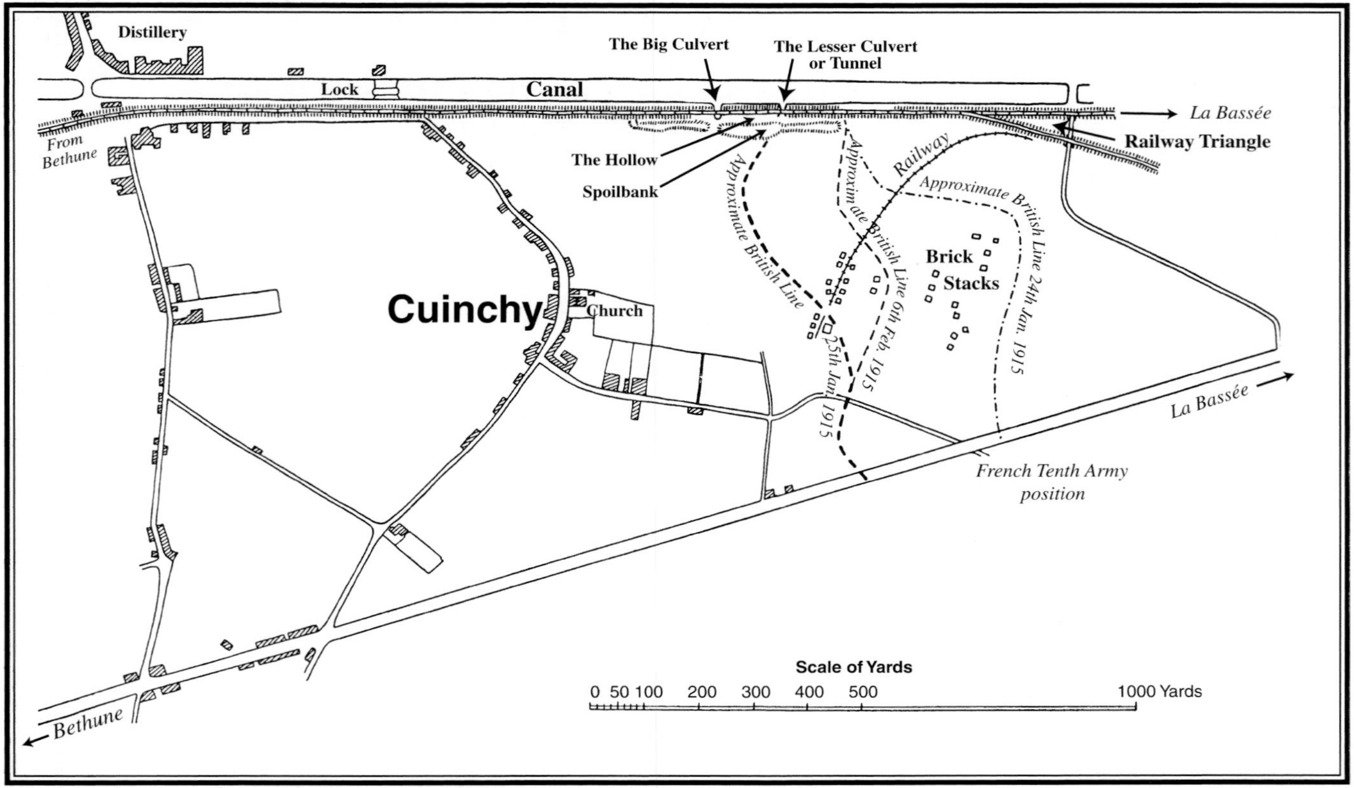

Cuinchy and the area where Michael O'Leary won his Victoria Cross

From Bethune

Distillery

Bethune

Lock

Canal

Cuinchy

Church

The Hollow
Spoilbank

The Big Culvert

The Lesser Culvert
or Tunnel

Approximate British Line

25th Jan 1915

Approximate British Line 6th Feb. 1915

Brick
Stacks

Approximate British Line 24th Jan. 1915

Railway

French Tenth Army
position

La Bassée

Railway Triangle

La Bassée

Scale of Yards

0 50 100   200   300   400   500   1000 Yards

56

Not once or twice in our rough island story
The path of duty was the way to glory.
Ode on the Death of the Duke of Wellington 1852

6

MICHAEL O'LEARY V.C. THE WILD COLONIAL BOY
1st Battalion The Irish Guards
Cuinchy, 1 February 1915

O N St. Patrick's Day, March 17 1916, King George V gave a short address at the annual parade of the Irish Guards for the presentation of shamrock to the officers and men of this elite regiment.[1] Expressing his pride and gratitude to the Guards for their endurance and fighting spirit in the present war the King singled out only one Guardsman by name:

In conferring the Victoria Cross on Lance Corporal – now Lieutenant – Michael O'Leary, the first Guardsman to win this coveted distinction, I was proud to honour a deed that, in its fearless contempt of death, illustrated the spirit of my Irish Guards.

This young Irishman from Inchigeelan, near Macroom, County Cork[2] had been summoned from the Dominion of Canada on the outbreak of war to rejoin the colours of his old regiment: the Irish Guards. Answering the call, he immediately sailed for Great Britain and on 22 October Michael O'Leary, trained soldier and skilled rifleman, was soon on a draft to France with the Ist Battalion Irish Guards. By the 23 November he found himself on a relatively quiet sector of the front line in Southern Flanders.

However, the 1st Battalion had suffered severe casualties that autumn in their heroic stand and arduous retreat from Mons, and again in early November at Ypres when, after 28 days of incessant fighting against heavy odds, the Battalion had come out of the line less than a company strong and with only four officers.

Guardsman O'Leary had arrived at the front in a strange time of transition for the British Army. Following such heavy losses in every sector, the British Expeditionary Force was undergoing a drastic reconstruction. As a regular army it had almost ceased to exist and the task of absorbing thousands of newly trained volunteer troops was in process. Even the problem of supplying these new armies with munitions, artillery and high explosives, had not yet been properly tackled by the War Office. The unique experience of truce and fraternisation with the enemy which occurred at Christmas only emphasised the comparative quiet along the British line. By early 1915 the British armies were still in no condition to take part in any prolonged offensive action: the battles of 1914 were over; those of Neuve Chapelle, Festubert and Loos still to come. In general, therefore, the advantage lay with the Germans and the best that could be hoped for was to secure every position by holding fast "at all costs", as Lord Cavan was to tell the Grenadiers at Givenchy. Bombing attacks and local assaults were the order of the day. It is said that the first "raid", which was to become such a persistent feature of trench warfare, first took place at this time.[3]

On 5 January 1915, Michael O'Leary was promoted to Lance Corporal and at the end of the month the 1st Battalion Irish Guards – part of Lord Cavan's 4th Brigade, returned to the line among the brickfields in the flat, open, marshy countryside south of the Bethune-La Bassée Canal, to a sector described unofficially as:

'not very wet but otherwise damnable.'

In contrast, one British Officer present had remarked rather naively:

The whole position is most interesting and requires a considerable amount of ingenuity.

Here, near the ruined village of Cuinchy, the British Line, already interlaced with underground workings, saps and communication trenches, ran through the brickfield and was overlooked by a high embankment and railway track. The brickfield itself was littered with several stacks of bricks, some thirty feet high: excellent for observation but a continual source of danger since few were in British hands and, in places, the occupying Germans were only ten feet away.

Suddenly the whole sector exploded. On 25 January, Crown Prince Rupprecht of Bavaria, with artillery support for his Bavarian Infantry, launched a ferocious attack from La Bassée to Aire on the south side of the Canal, and on the north side against the British positions at Givenchy. Realising that a local victory would be reported direct to the Kaiser himself, the Bavarians, with grim determination, swept over the British firing lines and took the village, only to be driven out slowly and relentlessly at the point of the bayonet. Even so, they continued to attack throughout the day against the north east corner until finally obliged to withdraw.

In marsh ground on the other side of the canal, five days of vicious attack and counter-attack along with trench loss and gain, often the result of bitter hand-to-hand fighting, saw the Germans still in possession of part of the trenches in the brickfields. As January came to an end the sector was still ablaze.

Along the canal the morning of 1 February dawned cold but fine. This was the day when Lance Corporal O'Leary was to prove his worth as a soldier and the Irish Guards were to be awarded their first Victoria Cross of the war. The situation that morning was grave. In the early hours the Germans had rushed and taken the forward trenches held by the 2nd Battalion Coldstream Guards. With all the officers either killed or wounded, C.Q.M.S. Canton, refusing to accept his orders to retire, hung on grimly with the remnants of his unexpected command. The 4th Battalion Irish Guards counter-attacked from neighbouring trenches but gained only a brief foothold.

The line had been broken however, and the position had to be retaken so that the line could be re-established. Giving orders that the ground was to be held at all costs, Lord Cavan left to arrange a bombardment from the howitzers and siege guns. At dawn the 1st Battalion Irish Guards, led by the remnants of the Coldstream, went in to action. A heavy barrage was followed by ten minutes rapid fire which blew away the parapet of the opposing trenches.[4] Then the assault went in. Fifty men of the 2nd Coldstream, followed by thirty men of No. 1 Company Irish Guards, carrying filled sandbags and two boxes of bombs with which to rebuild the barricade near the railway bridge, moved up through the Hollow.[5] It was here that Lance Corporal O'Leary saw and marked the site of a German machine gun post which had been set up on the Triangle during the night.

Realising at once the carnage amongst his comrades that it could cause, he decided to make straight for the gun. Away he went ahead of the rest and found himself in the corner of a German trench: a barricade in front of him. Although a formidable obstacle, the barricade together with its five enemy defenders proved no match for this lone Irishman. With his 'blood up', prompted by an awareness of the terrible danger facing his comrades, all five defenders were shot and O'Leary then set off in pursuit of the German machine gun crew further into the enemy positions. In full view and 'quite leisurely' said the unofficial report, he now progressed along the top of the embankment toward the crew who were frantically trying to reassemble their weapon which had been dismantled for the bombardment. Looming up right beside them, he killed three before returning with two prisoners whilst still intent upon killing another German to whom he had taken a dislike.

Astonishing though this episode was to the battalion, at the time to the man himself it was as natural as breathing. As a young constable in the Mounted Police in Regina, Saskatchewan, Michael O'Leary had apprehended two criminals engaged in an armed robbery; had fought a running gun battle with them before disarming and bringing them in as prisoners. On 1 February in Flanders he was a soldier in one of the proudest regiments of his country and with his unit facing a very dangerous situation, he had set off to do something about it and

The artist F. Matania's impression of Lance-Corporal O'Leary's award winning act of bravery

Michael O'Leary V.C.

London Gazette, 18 Feb., 1915:

Michael O'Leary, No. 3556, L.-Corpl., 1st Battn. Irish Guards. For conspicuous bravery at Cuinchy on 1 Feb. 1915. When forming one of the storming party which advanced against the enemy's barricades, he rushed to the front and himself killed five Germans who were holding the first barricade. After which he attacked a second barricade, though 60 yards further on, which he captured after killing three of the enemy and making prisoners of two more. L.-Corpl O'Leary thus practically captured the enemy's position by himself, and prevented the rest of the attacking party from being fired upon.

He was mentioned in Despatches in 1914 and 1915, and promoted Second Lieutenant, Connaught Rangers. Lieutenant O'Leary also received the Cross of St. George (Russia).

The recruitment poster featuring Michael O'Leary V.C.

achieved his singular objective. Spirited and immensely brave though it most certainly was, this was not the action of blind rage but the skill of a superb soldier: killing where necessary; taking prisoners when possible. To Michael O'Leary it was as simple as that. The battle entry of the Irish Guards was equally laconic:

This was a fine piece of work and he has been recommended for an award.

Immediate promotion in the field to Sergeant was followed by an official recommendation for the highest military honour Great Britain can give for special acts of valour : the Victoria Cross. On 18th February, just under three weeks later, the citation was published in the London Gazette and the Irish Guardsman from County Cork officially became Michael O'Leary V.C. As the unofficial report said so succinctly :

By his great gallantry he undoubtedly saved the two leading companies of the Coldstream and the Irish Guards many casualties.

By now the story of his exploit had spread through the regiment, through the brigade and through the army. In order to dispel rumours that he had been killed in action Sergeant O'Leary was given leave and as soon as he set foot in London, His Majesty King George V summoned him to Buckingham Palace and personally decorated him with the Victoria Cross. Overnight Sergeant O'Leary V.C. had become a national hero. It is difficult to understand the extent of the euphoria which broke over his head in the months that followed without an awareness of the political situation in Ireland at that time.

During the summer of 1914 while Michael O'Leary had been in Canada, the British army in Ireland was on the verge of mutiny.[7] The five armed forces and two armed police forces of the country were preparing to fight each other.[7] It was the knowledge of this very situation that had convinced the Germans that Great Britain could not become embroiled in any European conflict. However, the passing of the Home Rule Bill, which was now on the Statute books, had totally changed the scene.

When, on 3 August in the House of Commons Sir Edward Grey had announced the Government's decision to declare war on the Germans, the M.P. and leader of the Irish Nationalist Party at Westminster, John Redmond, impetuously rose to his feet and pledged complete allegiance to the Crown and Empire. Therefore, immediately following the Declaration of War, a wave of pro-British feeling swamped Ireland as large numbers of Irishmen began to enlist.[9] It was this change of heart which precipitated Sergeant O'Leary V.C. – the very epitome of Irish fighting spirit, into a national hero. His bravery appealed to a populace at a time when England and Ireland had come together to embrace the cause of European freedom. Sergeant O'Leary V.C. became a living symbol of that unity and he responded worthily to this calling. He became widely known as details of his exploit, together with an accompanying photograph of the man, appeared on recruiting posters for Irish regiments. Wherever he went in Ireland he was greeted with a right royal reception.

The Lord Mayor of Cork placed the £400 raised as a testimonial fund in the hands of trustees for the benefit of their gallant holder of the Victoria Cross. At an Irish demonstration in Hyde Park in July 1915 with T.P. O'Connor, M.P. and President of the United Irish League in London, Michael O'Leary was welcomed and cheered wildly by over a hundred thousand people.

With such publicity however, the direction of his army career was bound to change. He was never to return to the Western Front, though he spent a period at a Training School for Cadets at British Headquarters in France. Following this, he was commissioned a Second Lieutenant in the 1st Battalion Connaught Rangers and sent to Galway in Connaught in the west of Ireland, to take part in a recruiting drive for the regiment.

He was to finish the war as a Lieutenant in the Tyneside Irish Brigade. At an Irish National Flag Day in Newcastle-on-Tyne, organised to provide comforts for the men of Irish regiments, Irish prisoners of war and disabled soldiers, the Lord Mayor gave an opening address. Referring to the King's praise of the Irish Guards he went on to say:

If His Majesty had only known it, the Tyneside Irish Brigade was equal to that of the Irish Guards! Here was proof of that: O'Leary had left the Guards to join the Tyneside Irish.

Nothing can demonstrate more clearly the affection and respect shown by all present for Second Lieutenant O"Leary than his reception on this day. He was kept at the salute for several minutes because of the cheering as he rose to speak and nothing could more clearly illustrate both his humour and humility than his address to the appreciative audience. After thanking them for the very kind reception they had given him, saying that it was more than he expected even from the people of Newcastle, he added:

As you are all aware – I only did my duty and I feel very proud and honoured to have rendered such service for my King and country. [cheers] I am not much of a speaker [voices: 'a bit of a fighter though!'] and I have found out that the more speeches I make – the worse I get. [laughter and cheers] And I'll tell you I was at a dance last night so I don't feel too well today! [laughter].

Second Lieutenant Michael O'Leary, 1st Battalion, Connaught Rangers

Second Lieutenant O'Leary went on to do his duty, serving in Salonika and Macedonia with the Connaught Rangers, then attached to the 9th Indian Brigade, 3rd Indian Division; being mentioned twice in despatches and receiving the George Cross 3rd Class [Russia]. After the war he returned to England and was stationed in Dover barracks until he retired in 1921. For the time being a very fine record of military service had been completed.

The war in Europe was over but Ireland was not at peace. The Easter Week Rising in Dublin in the spring of 1916 led by poets, dreamers and idealists, had been crushed by British military force and the leaders executed. It had, after all, taken place as thousands of other Irishmen were moving up towards the Somme battlefield and mass graves.[10] But the aftermath of the Rising lit a flame in Ireland which would never be extinguished. Opinion now changed, as reflected in a poem by the poet George Russell, known as A.E.:

> Your dream has left me numb and cold
> But yet my spirit rose in pride,
> Re-fashioning in burnished gold
> The images of those who died,
> Or were shut in the penal call –
> Here's to you Pearse : your dream not mine,
> But yet the thought – for this you fell –
> Turns all life's water into wine.[11]

With the death of the two Redmond brothers: Major Willie Redmond killed in action near Wytschaete on 7 June 1917, and the weary, saddened and disillusioned John Redmond in March 1918, the Irish

National Party at Westminster had crumbled. Home Rule, suspended through the war, would be forgotten. Now four words rang through Ireland: "Sinn Fein" – "Ourselves Alone". December 1921 would see the establishment of the Saorstat Eireann: the Irish Free State with the same status as the Dominion of Canada. Ireland would now slide into a bitter civil war where men who had fought together for three years would fight against each other for the sake of an ideal: the Republic.

From a London, where disabled ex-soldiers were begging on the streets: from an Ireland in turmoil; Michael O'Leary left to start life again in Canada. He would be there only a few years, working for the Michigan Railway Police, before returning with his wife and family to London. His old loyalties to the fore – he commenced work for the British Legion, continuing in civilian life to serve his old comrades-in-arms. In addition, for many years distinguished visitors at the Mayfair Hotel would become accustomed to the unfailing courtesy and good humour of the tall, upright Irishman, so well known to them, who greeted then at the entrance and who was himself guest-of-honour at many military gatherings and functions. These were happy and stable years for the O'Leary family.

But war was to come again and in September 1939 Michael O'Leary left with the first waves of the British Expeditionary Force for France before transferring to the Pioneer Corps where he was put in charge of a prisoner of war camp in Southern England until 1945, when he was discharged from the army on medical grounds. Nothing demonstrates more clearly this fine soldier's devotion to duty than the record of these last years of military service in failing health.

Quiet years followed until, on 1 August 1961, Michael O'Leary died. May the life of this humble and compassionate soldier stand as a symbol for all those Irishmen who fought, lived and died with steadfast loyalty and allegiance to a cause greater than themselves.

> Here's to you, men I never met,
> But hope to meet behind the veil,
> Thronged on some starry parapet
> That looks down upon Inisfail,
> And see the confluence of dreams
> That clashed together in our night,
> One river born of many streams
> Roll in one blaze of blinding light!
> *A.E. – 'Salutation'*

Notes:

1. For a number of years Queen Alexandra had personally defrayed the cost of an annual gift on St. Patrick's Day of shamrock to the officers and men of this purely Irish regiment of Guards.

2. Son of Mr. and Mrs. Daniel O'Leary whose cottage is now a show place for tourists on their way to the shrine of St. FinBarre at Gougane Barra.

3. In Sir Douglas Haig's despatches he relates that :

One form of minor activity deserves special mention, namely, the raids or 'sutting-out parties" which are made at least twice or three times a week against the enemy's line. They consist of a brief attack, with some special object, on a section of the opposing trenches, usually carried out at night by a small body of men. The characters of these operations – the preparation of a road through our own and the enemy's wire – the crossing of the open ground unseen – the penetration of the enemy's trenches – the hand-to-hand fighting in the darkness and the uncertainty as to the strength of the opposing force – gives peculiar scope to the gallantry, dash and quickness of decision of the troops engaged; and much skill and daring are frequently displayed in these operations.

4. It was calculated that each of the 140 riflemen fired off 200 rounds in that astonishing 10 minutes and such figures were far from unusual in the B.E.F. in those days; no wonder the Germans thought they were faced by machine guns.

5. On the eastern sector towards La Bassée the diverging railway lines were designated 'The Railway Triangle' and the western fringe near the canal bridge, due to the configuration of the embankment, 'The Hollow'.

6. Known as The Curragh Mutiny, Sir Henry Wilson's diaries state that :'Sir John sent for us at 1 O'clock – directly after, all commanders-in-chief came into the Chief of the Imperial General's Staff room and told us that the Army was unanimous in its determination not to fight Ulster. This is superb.'

7. The armed forces involved were : The Irish Volunteers, The National Volunteers, The Ulster Volunteers, The Citizen Army, The British Army, The Royal Ulster Constabulary and The Royal Irish Constabulary.

8. On 2 November 1915, John Redmond M.P. rose in the House of Commons to give figures on Irish enlistment : 100,000 men from Ireland had enlisted since the outbreak of war to join 150,000 already in the forces.

9. One of the many such Irishmen who fought and died on the Somme for the cause of the European War was the leading Irish nationalist Thomas Kettle, a 2nd Lieutenant, 9th Battalion Royal Dublin Fusiliers. Like so many of his countrymen, his call to arms led to an unknown grave on the battlefields of the Somme and his name today can be found on the great Memorial to the Missing at Thiepval.

10. The name Pearse in this poem refers to Padraig Pearse, who read out the Proclamation of a Republic on the G.P.O. steps in Dublin, Easter Monday 1916.

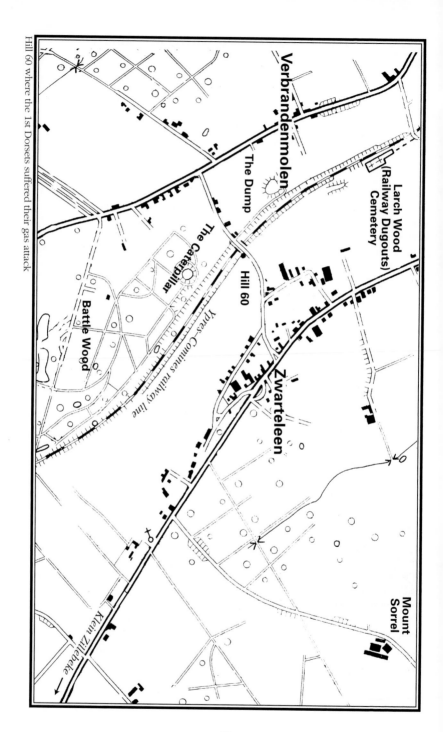

Hill 60 where the 1st Dorsets suffered their gas attack

Verbrandenmolen

The Dump

Larch Wood
(Railway Dugouts)
Cemetery

The Caterpillar

Hill 60

Ypres-Comines railway line

Battle Wood

Zwarteleen

Klein Zillebeke

Mount
Sorrel

"Souls of the slain! Souls of the slain! Where are these brave men now? In glass jam jars they had lifted sticklebacks out of every tributary of the Frome and Stour; they had "known for" cutty nests in churchyard walls; they had swung long surviving champion conkers on November afternoons when the aromatic smell of their father's bonfires was in the air and the first lamp-lit windows were showing down the street and on the green ...."

Llewelyn Powys – Somerset and Dorset Essays: Armistice Day 1932 .

7

NO PRISONERS FOR THE DORSETS
British troops first encounter gas at Hill 60
1st Battalion The Dorsetshire Regiment – 1st May 1915

O N THE 1 MAY 1915 the artificial mound in the Ypres Salient alongside the Ypres–Comines railway-line known as Hill 60 was in the sector of the 15th Brigade and held by the 1st Battalion The Dorsetshire Regiment under the command of Major H. N. R.Cowie.[1] This highly-regarded Commanding Officer was admired and respected by all ranks as a 'worker not a shirker' and accordingly, inspired a renewed *esprit-de-corps* amongst a depleted battalion which, like so many other units, had suffered extensive casualties throughout the first autumn of the war.

Major H. M. R. Cowie D.S.O.

Having held trench sectors south of Hill 60 throughout the early spring of 1915, on 29 April, the Dorsets moved forward to the sector on Hill 60 in relief of the 1st Battalion The Devonshire Regiment who duly retired into support positions in dug-outs around The Dump, another mound of spoil on the opposite side of the railway cutting. Captain and Adjutant Ransome describes their move up to the new positions in Larch Wood, a small wood sited alongside the same railway line a little to the north, as an "unpleasant experience". The Germans were employing a programme of harassing fire on The Dump, as well as on all roads, bridges and the cutting itself, to the rear. This was a well-known and predictable enemy tactic employed with the intention of both causing maximum disruption and establishing psychological superiority over incoming units to the line. One of the newly-promoted sergeants – C.S.M. Ernest Shephard of 'B' Company, mentions the perils faced by a ration party through this strafed terrain, when for nearly nine hours enemy fire followed them almost every step of the way and, in the process, ten 'good men' were lost. The nature of the ground itself is described by Captain Ransome:

> The support positions consisted of shelters dug into the hillside and covered with corrugated iron and sandbags. The term 'trench' has been used. Actually the defences were in the main breastworks constructed of sandbags with a parados in the rear. These 'trenches' were particularly deep and narrow in the Zwarteleen Salient. The continuous heavy fighting of the past fortnight had blotted out all landmarks and continually levelled breastworks. Digging on any scale was sure to disturb the bodies of British or German soldiers killed in the restricted area around the hill crest.

Trench 38 at Hill 60 in the spring of 1915. Men of the 1st Battalion Dorsetshire Regiment posing with a rifle periscope

At 3 p.m. on the following day, 30 April, 'A' and 'C' Companies, under the command of Captain Lilly and Lieutenant Butcher respectively, went on to the hill and took over all front line trenches. 'B' and 'D' Companies stayed in local reserve to the rear. Battalion Headquarters was established in Larch Wood.

With the recent use of gas by the Germans only two weeks before at St. Julian, British High Command had been thrown into a quandary over what form of protection could be supplied to the troops. Orders were issued for 'makeshift respirators' to be provided which consisted of men's suit flannel and gauze, with instructions that each man should 'wet it' should a gas cloud come over. As supplies began to make their way to selected troops in the line, all ranks were further advised that, if they had nothing better, a handkerchief should be dipped in water and placed over the mouth and nose and, where water was not available then urine would act as substitute. As Captain Ransome commented:

It is true to say that none of these expedients were of the slightest use[2]

As the Dorsets settled in to their new positions at dawn on the 1 May amidst heavy and continued shelling of the Dump, information received from the Devons on hand-over indicated the immense vulnerability of Trench 60 on the far side of the mine crater blown by the British two weeks beforehand. Here the proximity of the enemy front-line was down to a mere 40 yards. As a result of its forward and exposed position it was safe from enemy shelling but was consequently an easily accessible target for accurate sniping and random trench-mortar or hand-grenade attacks, which were continuous. The officer put in charge of this section of trench was the young 19-year-old Robin Kestell-Cornish, fresh from public school at Sherborne, Dorset. Lieutenant Butcher, commanding 'C' Company, occupied the parallel Trench 40 on the near side of the mine crater and Captain Lilly, commanding 'A' Company, occupied the right sector of adjoining trenches up to the railway line itself. For the remainder of the day the men were able to enjoy respite from enemy fire as, at about 4 p.m., all fell unusually quiet.

Then, close to 7 p.m., an enemy bombardment opened up on all positions across the hill and fifteen minutes later, before sentries could sound any form of warning thick white and yellow-green clouds were seen emerging from five hose-pipes opposite the length of front line across the entire sector. The battalion war diary succinctly outlines the position as found at approximately 7.30 p.m.:

The direction of the wind saved the garrison of 38, but the garrisons of 60, 43, 45 and 46 got the full benefit of the gas. The situation became critical.

Men who were alerted to the presence of gas reacted accordingly and, without informed instructions, crouched down in the bottom of the trenches in order to attempt to escape the deadly fumes. Unfortunately, this was a most ill-advised course of action; the concentration of the chlorine gas was so strong that scores of Dorsets were mortally affected by the fumes. C.S.M. Shephard explains :

First we saw a thick smoke curling over in waves from enemy trenches on the left. The cry was sent up that this was gas fumes. The scene that followed was heart-breaking. Men were caught by fumes and in dreadful agony, coughing and vomiting, rolling on the ground in agony.

Shephard relates escaping the worst effects of the gas by inhaling through a cloth soaked in water whilst exhaling through his nose.

While the gas was taking its effect rapid enemy fire opened up all along the line and shifted quickly to the railway cutting. The intention was clear – to prevent relief forces from the support trenches moving forward. However, men from 'A' and 'B' companies raced fearlessly in to the line in order to assist their fellow-Dorsets. Captain Lilly elucidates with his memories of this day:

My Company was the fortunate one as we were in the trenches with our

Captain C. O. Lilly

right on the railway cutting and when the gas came over just before dark it just missed the end of the trench my company were manning, but it got the rest of the battalion to a murderous extent. I cant remember the figures but I should say at least two-thirds of the battalion was gassed. I only know that I spent the rest of the night getting some sort of order into the trenches on my left. I don't want to go through such a night again, we had to lift dead and dying men out of the trench over the back of it, to enable my company to spread along the fire-step for any action that might be necessary. How I never got gassed myself I can't imagine, the buttons of my tunic were completely black from the chlorine, but I suppose that the gas being a heavy one, was dispersed by my moving up and down the trenches looking to see what had to be done and as I am tall, my head was more often than not above the top of the trench.

Back at Battalion Headquarters the first news of the presence of gas was telephoned through by Captain Hawkins of 'D' Company holding the Zwarteleen Salient. Hawkins' description of the situation as 'serious', allied to his personal doubt that he could 'hold their positions through the sheer incapacitation of their troops' was enough for Major Cowie to take instant and rather characteristic action. With the agreement of the Devons' C.O. Colonel Williams, six platoons were immediately sent forward in reinforcement, along with supports from the 1st Bedfordshire

Regiment. Major Cowie, feeling that his place was now in the front line along with his men, moved up to these positions, accompanied by Captain Ransome.

On the crest of the hill in Trench 60 Second Lieutenant Kestell-Cornish and his men were in dire peril. All officers were down and all but four of his men incapacitated from the initial effect of the gas with an imminent rush from the enemy expected. Then, in response to the situation pending a remarkably instinctive and courageous action took place. Using a piece of rifle flannelette soaked in water as protection against the overwhelming fumes, this gallant young subaltern accompanied by his four good men, seized rifles, jumped onto the parapet and opened fire into the cloud of poisonous gas billowing across their sector. The effect of this action was entirely intentional – the illusion was to give an impression that the trench was both fully-manned and strongly-held and thus, successfully, prevent an enemy onslaught across the small section of No Man's Land that separated the brief divide between the opposing forces. At virtually the same time Captain Batten of 'B' Company, having acted with enormous promptitude and qualities of leadership, arrived with a platoon having decided this to be the sector in greatest immediate need of assistance. Captain Ransome later calculated that the effect of Kestell-Cornish and his four assistants:

... was the factor which saved the day and ensured that the vital hill-crest remained in British possession. Their resistance just gave time for B Company to reach the hill-crest and take over and for the Devons to secure the salient.

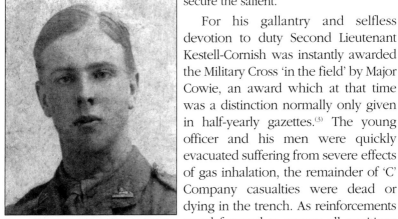
Second Lieutenant Kestell-Cornish M.C.

For his gallantry and selfless devotion to duty Second Lieutenant Kestell-Cornish was instantly awarded the Military Cross 'in the field' by Major Cowie, an award which at that time was a distinction normally only given in half-yearly gazettes.[3] The young officer and his men were quickly evacuated suffering from severe effects of gas inhalation, the remainder of 'C' Company casualties were dead or dying in the trench. As reinforcements raced forward to secure all positions on the hill, including Major Cowie and Captain Ransome, such was the unforgettable sight which awaited them. The evacuation of the wounded was proving extremely difficult and the notoriously deep, narrow trenches were clogged and choked with all manner of heavy casualties, all entirely due to the effects of gas and not one 'legitimate' casualty amongst them.

The machine-gun section, similarly, had ceased to exist, many now lying dead at their posts, killed by the gas. Among such mortalities was the well-liked and respected Sergeant Gambling, a character described by Ernest Shephard as a 'splendid fellow' and mentioned in several Dorsets' memoirs.[4]

Of those still alive but suffering the effects of gas poisoning it soon became clear that few were expected to recover. Horrified reinforcements bore witness to the appalling scene that greeted them and felt dreadful guilt and remorse at not being able to fully devote their time and attention to their wounded comrades whilst still in the throes of desperate defensive action and the organisation of vital communication and ammunition supplies. In an attempt to escape the continued perils of the gas fumes and seeking a place of safety and medical aid, many of the gas victims attempted to find their own way to safety and the rear, only to die anyway.

At the weakest point in the line – Trench 60 – the men were still under considerable pressure from strong enemy patrols launching grenade attacks on its flanks. All across the entire crest of the hill reinforcements bravely fought off such enemy assaults from trenches congested with dead, dying and severely wounded comrades. After some two hours, at around 9.30 p.m., Major Cowie declared the salient secured before returning to Headquarters where officers began to take stock of the situation and assess casualties. Of the Dorsets at their posts when the gas was released, 90 men had died from poisoning before receiving any medical aid. Of the 207 admitted to field ambulance a high proportion did not survive, 46 of them dying almost immediately at the dressing station. 32 other ranks were simply missing having crawled or staggered from the trenches in an attempt to reach a place of safety. C.S.M. Shephard states how the following morning patrols were sent out looking for them only to find nearly all of them dead. Captain Lilly explains how many of them had crawled back to Larch Wood's dugouts in order to hide from the gas:

By the morning things were not so bad and my company could go back into support, I think in a place called Larch Wood, to take stock of our situation. We had a further most unhappy task then, that was to find dozens of our men who had been gassed and had crawled back to hide themselves in various dugouts round about where they had died.

Of the total casualties – only two were described by the regiment as 'legitimate' – one man was killed and another wounded by shellfire.

As missing men were searched for the following day C.S.M. Shephard reflected on matters in his diary entry of Sunday, 2 May 1915:

The bitterest Sunday I have known or ever wish to know. My company lost one officer and 45 men mostly No.5 Platoon. 'C' Company lost all of 170 men except 38. Hardly know who is dead yet, but several of my best chums are gone under. Had we lost as heavily while actually fighting we would not have cared as much, but our dear boys died like rats in a trap, instead of heroes as they all were. The Dorset Regiment's motto now is 'No Prisoners!'. No quarter will be given when we again get to fighting. I feel quite knocked up, as we all are, and crying with rage.

Hill 60 quite apart from our losses is a terrible sight. Hundreds of bodies all over the place terribly mutilated, a large number of our own men, and larger number of Hun. Stench is awful as they cannot be buried, never quiet enough to do that. So they lie as they fell, silent spectators of modern warfare.

The following day whilst on picket duty, C. S. M. Shephard mentions finding yet more bodies in a barn close to the village of Zillebeke, and even farther back, almost in Ypres itself, and all dead. Even three days later the bodies of dead comrades were turning up in all manner of disused places. A graphic account of the entire day's action is contained in a letter written to his mother by Second Lieutenant Mansel-Pleydell, one of Captain Lilly's young officers in 'A' Company who had emerged from his dugout in Trench 39 to witness the unfolding events around him:

Company Sergeant-Major Ernest Shephard.

At about 7 o'clock I came out of my

dugout and saw a hose sticking over the German parapet, which was just starting to spout out a thick yellow cloud with a tinge of green in it. The gas came out with a hiss that you could hear quite plainly. I at once shouted to my men to put on respirators (bits of flannel) then I got mine and went and warned my captain, who did not know yet. Then the Huns began a terrible bombardment, not so much at us, but at our supports and our dressing station.

Now, either they had miscalculated the direction of the wind or else it had changed, for the gas did not come directly towards us but went slantwise, then our trench being so close the gas went into part of the German trenches as well as ours. They bolted from their when they got a whiff of the filthy stuff, a few of our men staggered away down the hill, some got into a wood behind it and died there, as the ground was low and the gas followed them, others only got as far as the mine head and communication trenches. The company in support on my left moved up into the firing line, as did also half of my platoon, consequently, I was left with a few men to do all the rescue work. My men were splendid; they all came with me into the gas, except the ones I ordered to stay behind, and we must have saved scores of lives. The men in most cases were lying insensible in the bottom of the trenches, and quite a number were in the mine head, which was the worst possible place. The best place after the first rush of gas was the firing line, being the highest point. I was the only officer not in the firing line and I should think quite two hundred men passed through my hands, some died with me and some died on the way down. I was simply mad with rage, seeing strong men drop to the ground and die in this way. They were in agonies. I saw two men staggering over a field in our rear last night, and when I went and looked for them this morning they were both dead.

The young officer, only 20 years old, concludes with chagrin:

I am absolutely sickened. Clean killing is at least comprehensive, but this murder by slow agony absolutely knocks me. The whole civilian world ought to rise up and exterminate those swine across the hill.[5]

So the first day of May came to an end, bringing with it a dawning realisation of the evolving methods of warfare, methods described by C.S.M. Shephard as 'barbarous', with the groans of scores of dying and badly wounded men combining with the ferocity of the fighting to create a chaos no worse than Hell itself.[6]

The men of the Dorsets might, in fairness, have expected to be withdrawn from the line in order to reassemble their surviving ranks and recover from their horrific ordeal. With the Devons now holding the front line, the Dorsets, still manning the support positions, awaited an anticipated period of rest normally granted under such circumstances. Such orders however, were not forthcoming and, instead, two days later on 3rd May, reinforcements duly arrived to swell their depleted ranks, leaving the entire unit to regroup as best they could. A somewhat embittered C.S.M. Shephard comments on the men's puzzlement at still finding themselves retained on active duty in this sector:

Why we are kept here after this severe blow is a mystery. It is high time our Division had a rest. We have now been in trenches and fighting with scarcely a break since 5th of April. Our Division has done all the fighting here on Hill 60 and have lost heavily in every regiment, yet still we plod on while there are supposed to be thousands of troops close by. Our casualties here at a low estimate are quite 400, and needless to say the men are very much shaken.[7]

During this time of adjustment, Captain Lilly experienced a chance discovery, the poignancy of which, affected him immensely in the years that followed. He found and recovered the body of a man, Second Lieutenant Jack Croft, who had been a friend of his brother at Cambridge. Lilly had recognised Croft's body lying near the edge of the crater just below the top of the hill, where it had been lying for two weeks. He recalls his hazardous endeavour in retrieving the body and eventually burying it further down the hill near the railway line:

I had a hell of a time getting him in and down the railway line to find a spot to bury him. We were sniped a good deal of the way. His body had been rifled of everything of value except a plain gold ring on the little finger of one hand and a few letters in his pocket, which I destroyed as soon as I got the address of the girl who had written them. I got into terrible trouble with Croft's father, an old parson, who I contacted when I got back to England myself, because I did not bring back to him everything his son had on him when he died. He simply had not the slightest idea of war and Hill 60 in particular, but as he was half demented with grief, I could not take any notice.[8]

By the 4 May, the Devons were relieved from their 3 day spell in the front line by the 2nd Battalion Duke of Wellington's (West Riding) Regiment and, as Senior Ranking Officer in this sector, Major Cowie accordingly assumed overall command although, regrettably this was destined to be extremely short-lived. At 5.45 a.m. on the following morning of 5 May, whilst returning from a visit to his new troops in the front line, Major Cowie was severely wounded by a fragment from a shell which burst near the entrance of the aid post within yards of the dug-out being used as Battalion Headquarters. This warm-hearted man, so beloved by the battalion, did not survive his wound and died, two weeks later, whilst back in England.[9]

As a well-liked and respected Commanding Officer, the loss to the battalion of the wounded Major Cowie was a bitter blow to the Dorset men, being felt, as it was, throughout the ranks. However, imminent dramatic developments were to afford the men little time in which to absorb their misfortune. Just three hours later, at around 8.45 a.m., startled troops of the 2nd Duke Of Wellington's in the Dorsets' old front line on the hill, witnessed the onset of a secondary gas attack this time of far greater planning and efficiency. With no precursory bombardment, the front line positions were quickly filled with heavy concentrations of gas pouring laterally along the trenches and their flanks, rapidly overpowering its unprepared occupants.

Within fifteen minutes Acting Commanding Officer Captain Batten and Captain Ransome received a message at Dorset Battalion Headquarters from the signal sergeant, warning them: "Gas coming over" followed by a subsidiary message: "They are all coming back."

On stepping out into the railway cutting Ransome's worst fears were confirmed: scores of gassed and demoralised troops were pouring down the cutting from the hilltop, dazed and bewildered, leaving the front line virtually abandoned. Moving at a slow pace and without panic, the troops' demeanour was likened by Ransome to:

... that of a football crowd leaving the ground at the end of an important match which the home team had unexpectedly lost.

Immediate and decisive action was called for if the entire hilltop sector and the cutting was not to be conceded to the enemy. From front support positions the word had already been passed around the men "Pads on, gas coming over" and, donning their equipment, the Dorsets anticipated orders to reinforce the 2nd Duke of Wellington's, still continuing to move slowly back down the hill. Under the command of Captain Lilly, 'A' Company, including its contingent of new reinforcements, were ordered to move forward and re-occupy trenches 38 and 39 from whence, it was hoped, the situation on the hillcrest itself could be ascertained. 'B', 'C' and 'D' Companies, who had lost so heavily on 1 May, were to remain in reserve under the command of Lieutenant Clayton.

Enemy shelling increased in intensity and, once again, moved southward in order to both maximise casualties amongst the retiring troops and also severely disrupt or prohibit any reinforcement manoeuvres. As a result, all telephone lines to both the front and rear of Dorset Battalion Headquarters were cut. The advancing Dorsets of 'A' Company were out on their own. As the men moved forward through the cloud of gas and retiring troops towards their old positions on the hill, their ability in facing, once more, this new adversary in the knowledge of its effects on their comrades from their recent experience, is a mark of the immense bravery of these good men.

On approaching the nearer of the two objectives – Trench 39, Captain Lilly was able to quickly assess the situation. Much of the trench was empty but, farther ahead, in Trench 38, the enemy was not only clearly visible but beginning to extend across towards other surrounding positions. From these elevated vantage points, if taken by the enemy, further hostile assaults on support and reserve positions would be almost assured. Lilly reached Company Headquarters – a dug-

The stone bridge spanning the railway cutting.

out on the side of the cutting between trenches 39 and 38 , in order to attempt to telephone Battalion Headquarters back in Larch Wood with a report of his findings. However, before he could discover that no such report could be made with communications still down, a splinter from a British shell ricocheted off the stone bridge immediately ahead of him and lodged itself in his arm. The shells from the British 4.5. batteries had been falling short for some time and had regrettably disabled the captain.[10]

2nd Lieut. H.G.M. Mansell-Pleydell M.C.

Taking charge of the situation, the young Second Lieutenant Harry Mansel-Pleydell immediately assumed command of the Company and set about deploying the men in a lateral advance along Trench 39. Although himself wounded by shrapnel glancing across his temple, Mansel-Pleydell was determined to drive the enemy from the trenches and vigorously conducted the rest of the entire day's action of the Dorsets, as described by Ernest Shephard:

When we arrived the Germans were in 38 trench, jumping on to Hill 60 and running along 39 to drive us out. We slung up a barricade nearly at left end of 39 where Germans were running towards us, and picked them off nicely there, some we bayoneted. This held the left of 39. Next we lined a communicating trench at right end of 39 and made things so hot for enemy in 38 that they retired from that trench. A Company then ran round the extreme right of 39 leading to 38 and bayoneted all who were still there. This left the Germans in possession of Hill 60.'

Having now secured Trench 38 and the greater part of 39, the Dorsets sent to Brigade for assistance whilst holding their positions. The enemy meanwhile, were pushing on through between the Dorsets and other units, further in to the Zwarteleen Salient where they now held trenches 40, 41, 42 and 43. The Dorsets were holding out but, to add to their problems, shells were dropping short and landing amongst the men, causing many casualties.

At Battalion Headquarters the Adjutant Captain Ransome was in overall command due to the incapacitation of Captain Batten from ga fumes. As telephone lines to Trench 38 were repaired, Ransome received a report of the severity of the situation indicating that assistance was urgently required. When the Captain also witnessed parties of Germans beginning to infiltrate down the valley to Zillebeke, he reasoned that if this movement continued in force then not only would Battalion HQ soon be at risk but that, ultimately:

... there seemed to be nothing, either in the shape of troops or trenches to prevent the enemy from pressing on into Ypres itself.

Ransome therefore decided to use the troops remaining under Lieutenant Clayton's command to form a defensive flank, only to discover that these troops had already followed 'A' Company up to the front line without orders. Accordingly, such men from Battalion Headquarters as could be spared, along with partially wounded victims of the attack, were moved into positions where they could bring fire to bear towards the north, thus covering any gaps in the forward positions. And so the situation, tenuous and vulnerable, awaited the arrival of reinforcements. The Dorsets must stand fast if the line was to be held.

Then, at about 11 a.m. when lines to Brigade Headquarters were reinstated, a message came through that the Cheshires were coming up and that the Commanding Officer, Lieutenant-Colonel Scott, would take over command of the sector.

However, Lieutenant-Colonel Scott was killed almost at once on reaching Larch Wood and his second-in-command took over. The Cheshires, advancing against the enemy positions and strengthening the Dorsets in their trenches, also dealt with the enemy that had broken through as far as Zillebeke but by 1 p.m. when it became clear that the Germans would not be ejected from the Zwarteleen Salient, the Cheshires, assisted by the 6th Battalion Kings (Liverpool Regiment), began digging in and consolidating their positions opposite the enemy. Trench 39 was prolonged and eventually recaptured in its entirety and most of trenches 40, 41, 42 and 43 were cleared by bombing attacks which had made good progress in spite of the German stick grenades' superiority to that of the British 'jam tin'.

It was during this period of activity that a most regrettable casualty occurred when another subaltern from 'A' Company, Second Lieutenant George Shannon, was killed. Second Lieutenant Arthur Greg, a Subaltern of the 1/5th Cheshire Regiment in Trench 40, recalls the problems encountered in responding to the copious German grenades

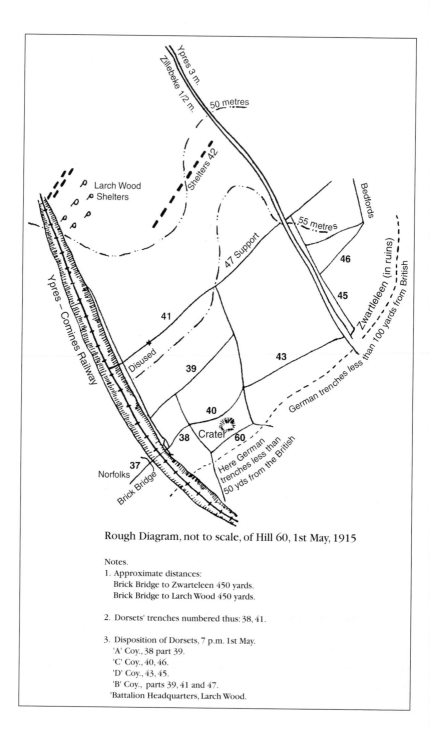

Rough Diagram, not to scale, of Hill 60, 1st May, 1915

Notes.

1. Approximate distances:
   Brick Bridge to Zwarteleen 450 yards.
   Brick Bridge to Larch Wood 450 yards.

2. Dorsets' trenches numbered thus: 38, 41.

3. Disposition of Dorsets, 7 p.m. 1st May.
   'A' Coy., 38 part 39.
   'C' Coy., 40, 46.
   'D' Coy., 43, 45.
   'B' Coy., parts 39, 41 and 47.
   'Battalion Headquarters, Larch Wood.

being thrown over the barricades and sandbags. The Germans were superior in both numbers and in their reconnaissance of the new positions of both sides. Having been ordered to 'hold on' and with additional perils of heavy enemy cross fire, Second Lieutenant Greg made desperate pleas for fresh supplies of grenades to stem the flow of the enemy onslaught. At approximately an hour before dusk he recalls:

... an officer of the Dorsetshire Regiment had his head blown off just as he was handing me a new box of grenades. I felt very upset as I felt that somehow I was to blame for having urgently demanded more grenades.[11]

As dusk approached and both sides began to tire, the intensity of the day's fighting subsided and the wounded were able to receive assistance although Ernest Shephard, himself now suffering from gas inhalation, recalls:

Most pitiable scenes, several men died in my own arms as I was helping them! ... it was a perfect Hell, shelled from front and by our own artillery in rear. The enemy's bombs, rifle fire etc... the fear of more gas. Were ever human beings asked to endure such as this before? We were of course hourly expecting to be relieved. We were all exhausted.

Larch Wood near Hill 60. Battalion Headquarters of the 1st Battalion Dorsetshire Regiment was based here in the spring of 1915

Captain A. L. Ransome

At dusk the situation was reviewed by Captain Ransome who surmised that the Dorsets and Cheshire Regiment held trenches 38, 39 and most of 40 – the enemy: Trench 60 and the Zwarteleen Salient. In spite of continued efforts, including a counter-attack at 10 p.m. by two battalions of the 13th Brigade – the 2nd Battalion King's Own Scottish Borderers and 1st Battalion Royal West Kents, any progress in clearing out the enemy from their positions failed. Due to the combined difficulties of darkness impeding most reconnaissance over the hostile terrain and the lack of artillery support the main objective remained the consolidation of the day's gains.

In the early hours of the following morning, 6 May, the Dorsets were finally withdrawn from their positions on the hill and marched back to the dugouts and bivouacs they had left a week beforehand at Kruisstraat, arriving at 4 a.m.: a journey described by Ernest Shephard as 'very weary'. In the space of just one week at Hill 60 the battalion, which had gone into the line some 700 strong, now numbered just 173 all ranks.[12] Having endured both gas attacks and the ensuing fighting for possession of the hill, nearly all survivors were either exhausted or affected by exposure to the gas, or both.

Many individuals had distinguished themselves in the fighting, among them – Second Lieutenant Mansel-Pleydell, acting C.O. of 'A' Company, whose strong qualities of leadership in directing the successful recapture of trenches on the Hill by his men, deservedly earned him the Military Cross.[13] In the aftermath of their action here, the 1st Battalion Dorsets achieved a well-founded reputation for their 'fine fighting', as reflected in their battle honours. Such good men as these had relatively little preparation for the full extent of their endurances on Hill 60 and yet, had borne its vicissitudes with initiative, courage and fortitude. Captain Ransome's privately printed account of the battle cannot disguise his pride at his men's conduct:

Hill 60, on the 1st May, 1915, was the Dorsets' battle; the whole weight of the gas attack fell upon them; and they did not fail. In spite of their experiences on that day they did not hesitate for a moment when, five days later, they saw another unit, demoralized by gas fumes, streaming away to the rear. They faced again the forbidden weapon in the full knowledge of what its effects could be, either a painful death or severe illness with possible lasting after-effects. Led by the four gallant officers – Lilly, Shannon, Mansel-Pleydell and Clayton, they went forward through the gas cloud to their old positions on the Hill and remained at grips with the Germans throughout that long day, shelled sometimes by their own artillery and facing an enemy flushed with success and armed with hand grenades, so important in trench fighting, which were superior to their own. They held all their gains until relieved at night.

Notes:

1. Hill 60, so named from the ringed contour marking it on the maps at the time, was not a natural feature of the land; it was a spoil bank formed by earth excavated when the railway cutting had been made in the Nineteenth Century. Re-taken from German possession by the British in their attack on the 17 April, the hill was an understandable military target for occupation because of its strategic importance to the surrounding Flanders' Plain and close proximity of Ypres itself, just some 3 miles to the north.

2. The first gas masks issued to the Dorset troops arrived in June 1915, a month after the first gas attack. Captain Ransome describes the issue as: "a simple contrivance, a flannel bag which had been saturated in a glycerine solution, and it was pulled over the head, the ends being tucked beneath the coat collar; it was filled with glass eye-pieces and a tube to exhale the breath. Every man carried two smoke helmets, as they were called, in a satchel slung over his shoulder."

3. In a recruiting address at Bournemouth in June 1915, Captain Bullock, Adjutant of the 5th Dorsets, spoke to the assembled gathering of the 'Gallant Dorsets who had the honour, if such it could be called, of being the first to knock up against the Germans' poisonous gas. One incident during the fighting called for mention. A young Lieutenant of only 19 had, with the assistance of 4 men, held a trench against the enemy – for they knew if they had given way the hill would have been lost. The lieutenant was awarded the M.C. on the field without any waiting and recommendations to the War Office.'

Robert Vaughan Kestell-Cornish was evacuated to hospital on 3rd May suffering from the effects of gas inhalation but after only a week's recuperation and against doctors' advice to return to England, he returned to the Battalion and took over the duties of Adjutant. Although strenuously supported as a Victoria Cross candidate by Major Cowie and other senior ranking officers of the Brigade, there was immense disappointment amongst the Battalion when this was not granted. Receiving continued acclaim as a respected and competent officer with 'unique gifts of leadership' in one so young, Second Lieutenant Kestell-Cornish, M.C. and Bar, was eventually appointed G.S.O.3 of the 32 Division in August 1917. He died of wounds in 1918 and is buried in Boulogne Eastern Cemetery. He was a personal friend of fellow 1st Battalion officer Lieutenant Charles Douie, author of *The Weary Road*.

4. Sergeant Charles Gambling D.C.M. was one of the original contingent of the Regiment which had arrived in France in August 1914. Sergeant Gambling was one of many soldiers buried around Hill 60 but whose graves were destroyed and lost in the subsequent fighting. His name is commemorated on the Menin Gate Memorial to the Missing.

5. Second Lieutenant Mansel-Pleydell's mother had her son's letter published in the May 27th edition of the East Dorset Herald newspaper, 1915.

6. Major Billy Congreve witnessed some of the casualties whilst at Bailleul on 2nd May. He described the men as: "... very bad indeed, so bad that the doctors are hardly able to save a single case. Oxygen is but little use, and they just get more and more acute and die. Some turn quite purple – horrid to see. It was fearful seeing the rows and rows of stretchers in the yard, all gasping in misery,"

7. Over a month later C.S.M Shephard was still wondering why he and his men had not been withdrawn to rest. His diary entry for 12 June 1915, reflects: "We have been expecting to go back for a rest, but today we are told we go to trenches again tomorrow. Where is this tremendous new army the papers blow so much about? Is it a phantom army, and when in the name of common sense are we to be relieved? Apparently we shall do another 20 days from now, making a total of 44 days without a relief. These are questions I ask myself. Can find no solution. Apparently the responsible authorities will get the very last ounce out of us. They can have mine, but the men complain a good deal, and I have to stifle my opinion and rebuke them."

8. In 1927 Captain Lilly returned to the old fighting ground of Hill 60. Lilly writes how: "some ten years later I did go up that railway to see if I could find Croft's grave, but the ground had been so mangled with shells etc.. I could hardly find Hill 60, let alone a corner of a foreign field which is for ever England. I don't wonder that the War Graves Commission could not find many thousands of graves in that area. I must have buried at least twenty or thirty of my company between Hill 60 and the Bluff. All that ground ten years later was a complete wilderness, all the landmarks I had known had ceased to exist." The officer whom Captain Lilly had buried was Second Lieutenant John A.C. Croft 4 Royal Warwicks attached 2nd West Riding. Today, like so many others who fell in this area, Jack Croft has no marked grave and is commemorated on the Menin Gate. He was killed in action on the Hill on 18 April 1915.

9. Major Norman Cowie is buried in West Woodhay Churchyard, Berkshire. His death was described by Captain Ransome as 'the Regiment's heaviest loss in the whole war'. At the height of the fighting on May 1st, Major Cowie was actively participating in driving the enemy back by bomb throwing alongside his men.

10. In his memoir Captain Lilly comments that it took over a year before the piece of shattered bone worked its way out of his arm and he was free of abscesses. This

effectively ended Lilly's war as far as the Dorsets were concerned.

11. In forwarding Second Lieutenant Shannon's Military Cross to his father, the Secretary of State for War expressed his regret that the officer: 'had been killed before being able to receive his award in person from the hands of His Majesty the King'. Having already been Mentioned in Despatches on 16 February 1915, for gallant and distinguished conduct in the field, Second Lieutenant Shannon had been awarded the Military Cross on 18 February, two days later.

Second Lieutenant George Shannon is buried in Larch Wood (Railway Cuttings) Cemetery.

12. C. S. M. Ernest Shephard's compassionate approach toward his men and his professional commitment to his soldiering is evident throughout his diaries, published under the title of 'A Sergeant Major's War'. In November 1916 he left G.H.Q. Cadet School near St. Omer as a Second Lieutenant and was posted to the 5th Battalion Dorsetshire Regiment. Second Lieutenant Shephard was killed in action near Beaucourt on 11 January 1917, and is buried in A. I. F. Burial Ground, Flers.

Battalion casualties for the 5 May were: 1 officer and 14 OR killed, 3 officers and 48 OR wounded, 3 officers and 60 OR gassed, 1 officer and 48 OR missing. Total casualties incurred in the Hill 60 fighting: 513 all ranks.

12. With the departure of Captain Lilly from the Battalion, Second Lieutenant Mansel-Pleydell was promoted to Lieutenant and given full command of 'A' Company, where he became a much-valued and respected commanding officer. Sadly, he only survived another 12 months of the war. In the following May of 1916, on the Somme battlefield, he lost his life in the grounds of the old Thiepval Château whilst on an intelligence reconnaissance of No Man's Land in front of the Hammerhead Sap. Educated at Marlborough College, Wiltshire, he had written to a master at the College after his engagement at Hill 60, dismissing his injury as a 'close shave'. The citation for the Military Cross for his action on 5 May praises his:

... gallantry and ability .... Although wounded early in the attack, he commanded his platoon in the trenches [which had been vacated by the unit holding them in the morning] with great skill and coolness, and later took charge of the whole of his company after his captain had been wounded. It was largely due to him that a considerable length of trench, which had been occupied by the enemy, was gradually regained.

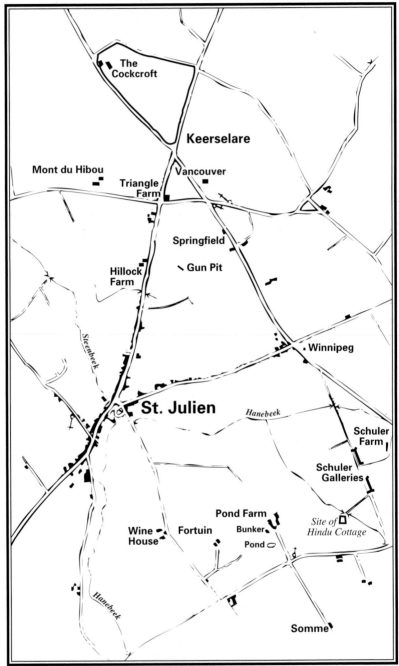

The Operation Cockcroft strongpoint objectives north of St. Julien

Nothing in this world is so powerful as an idea whose time has come.
Victor Hugo.

8

TANKS AT ST JULIEN
Operation Cockcroft
Ypres, 19 August 1917

THE CLUSTER OF FARMS around the crossroads above the village of St. Julien due north of Ypres, represents an industrious community centred around and busily involved with agriculture, yet twice during the traumatic war years of 1914-1918 it was the centre of something far more sinister. In April of 1915 the 1st Canadian Division was thrust into the line here to fill the gap caused by the first use of gas by the Germans and, in the summer of 1917, shortly after the opening of Third Ypres, a classic tank and infantry action took place in the vicinity, overcoming several of the well-defended redoubts around this vital road junction. These redoubts had withstood a number of British infantry assaults, which had been mounted to maintain pressure on this sector with a view to breaking through and opening the way to the villages of Langemarck and Poelcappelle, two major bastions in the hands of the enemy.

A well-planned and successfully implemented attack, using tanks and specially-trained supporting infantry, had eventually subdued these strongly-garrisoned forts with a surprisingly low casualty rate for the attackers. These previously impenetrable strongpoints were taken with total losses to the British infantry of only fifteen men wounded, and with tank crew casualties of two killed and twelve wounded, and yet the estimated casualty rating before the battle was 1,000 men. Success had been achieved with a perfect blend of tactics, and this successful action had enabled an advance of 600 yards over a mile of front.

During Third Ypres the ground fought over was aptly described as "the world's worst battlefield". Ypres had once been an inland port and, although the surrounding land had been reclaimed, the Flemish water levels were never far below the surface. By 1917 the two warring armies, with the help of the incessant rain, destroyed water-courses and devastated countryside, had reduced the environs of Ypres to a veritable swamp where men, animals and equipment frequently sank in the mud to disappear without trace.

Whereas the opening of the main offensive on 31 July 1917, had proved successful, German resistance soon stiffened and, with effective counter-attacks around St. Julien, they had brought the British movement to a halt. British High Command ordered resumption of the attack, using the tanks and supporting infantry in an action toward the general direction of Poelcappelle in what some perceived would become a bloody battle of attrition in the muddy swamp-lands.

The action against five of the redoubts, The Cockcroft, Mont du Hibou, Triangle Farm, Hillock Farm and Gun Pit, a conglomeration of concrete gun-emplacements sited on just east of Hillock Farm, across the St. Julian–Poelcappelle road, would be launched as *Operation Cockcroft*, named after the most northerly of the group of strongpoints, at Zero hour, 4.45 a.m., 19 August.

The country across which the tanks were to travel was in a condition exactly opposite to that needed for the efficient use of such cumbersome machines, and it would be equally as difficult to traverse for the infantry designated to follow them. Nevertheless, the battle route had been well conceived, being carefully selected – chosen and pre-prepared with the squadron's weight and speed in mind. The Royal Engineers constructed special crossings to bridge the Steenbeek, one of the many deep streams snaking across the Flemish countryside, and progress northward along the road from St. Julien to Poelcappelle would be screened by heavy artillery, shrapnel and smoke barrages. The starting point was situated at the beginning of this road leading north out of St. Julien, but, although screened from the enemy by a left-hand bend just before the road straightened out on its long route to Poelcappelle, it ran directly into enemy lines and the tank would have to run a gauntlet of fierce opposition immediately on turning the bend.

Up to this time in the war, tanks had not exactly covered themselves with glory in action and, to British High Command and military leaders in general, they were only taken into consideration for use as a last resource. In previous actions further south, along the Menin Road near Sanctuary Wood, some had broken down or found themselves bogged in the ground conditions totally unsuitable for their forward movement. Others, using untested tactics, had fallen-foul of German anti-tank guns astutely placed around Clapham Junction, east of Hooge, picking-off the heavy, slow moving machines at will. So many of them were disabled and stranded in the area that it earned itself the name 'Tank Graveyard'. However, to the relief of Brigadier-General Elles, the young commander of this new arm, his chief, General Sir Ivor Maxse, was one of the few senior commanders who had any faith in the weapon, and who felt disposed to give the machines another chance to prove their worth in action during Third Ypres.

The German redoubts to be attacked were large, concrete-structured fortifications, some of them with walls eight-feet thick in places, and garrisoned by anything up to 100 men each. Some were sited either side of the St. Julien–Poelcappelle road with others forming a rough triangle at its northern end, all making up part of the large network of strongpoints dominating this north-eastern area of the Ypres sector of Flanders. Heavily fortified, each housed numerous machine-gun teams and were surrounded by a system of trenches, outposts and wire-entanglements. They had proved to be impregnable stumbling blocks to the many infantry attacks directed at them to date, and all attempts to make headway here had resulted in heavy losses for the attacking British forces.

The Tank Graveyard at Hooge

A British tank being loaded aboard ship for transportation to France.

A composite company of fourteen tanks from 'G' Battalion, 1st. Brigade, Tank Corps, was to spearhead the operation, attacking on the British 11th and 48th Divisional fronts. The original Brigade order detailed use of the fourteen tanks as: eight for attack purposes, four to act in reserve and two to work as supply tanks. This order was later adjusted to use only eleven tanks: two to target The Cockcroft, two to take on Mont du Hibou, two for Triangle Farm, two for Hillock Farm and Gun Pit, one for just the Gun Pit and to operate as 'Moppers-up' and two to be held in reserve and to act as further 'Moppers-up'. These last two were to stay in position at the California Trench mustering area. Two companies of infantry from the 144th and 145th Brigades, 48th Division would allocate units to support the tank company and to occupy the redoubts on their front as the tanks cleared them, with troops of the 33rd Brigade, 11th Division supporting the assault on The Cockcroft, the most northerly.

During the night of 18 August, the eleven tanks left the California Trench mustering area rumbling forward northeast of Wieltje, moving, in line, up the road to their starting point on the stretch of road immediately north of St. Julien. The tanks, commanders and their allocated objectives were:

Tank No.	Commander	Objective	Remarks
G.4	Lt. J. D. Willard	The Cockcroft	Male
G.45	2/Lt. H. G. Coutts	The Cockcroft	Female
G.29	2/Lt. A. G. Baker	Mont du Hibou	Male
G.32	Lt. E. T. Morgan	Mont du Hibou	Female
G.31	2/Lt. C. R. H. Kane	Triangle Farm	Female
G.28	2/Lt. A. V. Close	Triangle Farm	Female
G.52	2/Lt. H. H. Claughton	Hillock Farm + Gun Pit	Female
G.47	2/Lt. D. G. Browne	Hillock Farm + Gun Pit	Female
G.44	2/Lt. E. H. J. Chaddock	Gun Pit and Mopper-up	Female
G.53	2/Lt. J. S. Bubb	Mopper-up	Bt. Res.
G.10	2/Lt. A. E. Jukes	Mopper-up	Bt. Res.

Problems were experienced as soon as the advance began. Tank G.31, ditched *en route* and took no part in the action. Another, G.4, developed radiator trouble, causing two of its crew members to collapse. This tank took up position at the rear of the column and hobbled along in its own time.

Nevertheless, at Zero hour, 4.45 a.m. on 19 August, the eight attacking tanks left the starting point and advanced along the St. Julien–Poelcappelle road, moving in-line ahead, and on up the straight, now mud-slimed pavé road, those with their objectives being the farthest north leading the column. Even though the promised artillery barrage of heavy artillery, shrapnel and smoke did its best to protect and screen their movement, the tanks came under enemy fire immediately, the starting point being only about 400 yards from the enemy lines. The tanks, in their turn, returned the compliment, firing with all they had, sweeping both sides of the road with Lewis machine gun fire.

Hillock Farm was quickly dealt with by tanks G.52 and G.44 who, once the British infantry had occupied it, then turned their attention to the Gun Pit, each firing 400 to 500 rounds from their machine guns. This position was soon consolidated by the supporting infantry, the enemy occupants last seen running in an easterly direction, helped on their

A ditched tank at St. Julien in October 1917

way by a stream of machine gun bullets from G.47 which, having swapped objectives with G.44, until then had given its full attention to clearing the Gun Pit on the opposite side of the road. The mission completed, G.47, followed by its sisters G.52 and G.44, then made its way back to base, the job done and with no casualties other than those of the dispirited enemy.

Meanwhile, G.4, with its damaged radiator, had made its slow way up the same road, heading for its target, The Cockcroft. It also engaged Hillock Farm and the Gun Pit on its way, but never made it to The Cockcroft. Six of its crew fell unconscious due to engine fumes caused by its damaged radiator. Its commander, Lieutenant J. D. Willard, was wounded while walking outside the tank trying to get some fresh air. Driver Parkinson dragged his commander back into the tank and, enlisting the aid of one of the troops from the supporting 1/8th Worcestershires, drove back to St. Julien where the tank then ditched. G.4's part in the action was over – it had taken four and a half hours to complete its round trip from the starting point at St. Julien.

G.32 had made its way up the road to reach the left turn that would take it to the menacing Mont du Hibou, a sizable two-storied classic example of German architecture. It had also let loose a hail of bullets at Hillock Farm and the Gun Pit as well as at a number of machine gun posts and dugouts sited either side of the road. G.29, its sister targeting Mont du Hibou, had missed the turning and was firing directly at the strongpoint from the Poelcappelle Road from where it had ditched, skidding into the cloying mud and slime. G.32 blasted away at the Mont du Hibou back entrance, driving out about 30 of the occupants who were quickly rounded-up by the 1/8th Warwickshires, the supporting infantry. G.29, which had been firing non-stop into the front entrance from its ditched position alongside the Poelcappelle road, sank deeper and deeper into the mud until it could no longer elevate its gun. After six and a half hours of action the commander, Second-Lieutenant A. G. Baker left the tank, formed his crew into Lewis gun teams, and joined the Warwicks in consolidating the position..

In the meantime G.28, on its way to Triangle Farm, had also let the occupants of Hillock Farm and the Gun Pit know that it was passing by, letting loose with its full complement of machine guns. Unfortunately the tank commander, Second-Lieutenant A. V. Close, was wounded in the hand and, unable to work the brakes, caused the tank to slip off the road into deep mud where it firmly embedded itself. It was immediately fired upon from four enemy machine guns which knocked-out five of its Lewis guns. The crew stayed inside for 16 hours before removing a turret to get out and make their way back to base – but not before disabling the tank by destroying its clutch with a Mills bomb. Two members of the crew as well as Second-Lieutenant Close, were wounded in this action.

Triangle Farm proved to be a formidable obstacle and was only taken after British infantry entered it and bayonetted or captured the garrison. Tank G.45, like the rest of the attack squadron, blasted away at anything that looked like it belonged to Germany while on its way up the road to The Cockcroft, including of course, Hillock Farm and the luckless garrison of the Gun Pit. It quickly engaged The Cockcroft and in no time at all the garrison gave up the fight and left in a rush, many being killed by the spirited and spitting machine guns of G.45, which had managed to ditch itself during the action. The commander, Second-Lieutenant H. G. Coutts, left the tank and, not seeing his supporting

Hillock Farm today on the left-hand side of the St.Julien–Poelcappelle road. This photograph was taken from the approximate position of Gun Pit on the other side of the road, a site of which there is no longer any visible trace

The long road just past the mustering pont north of St. Julien that the tanks followed. Hillock Farm can be seen on the left, but of Gun Pit, to the right, there is no trace, although its position is well marked on trench maps of the time.

infantry, sent two of his men to find them. He then set-up his crew in Lewis gun lines, maintaining a watch over his prized Cockcroft. His men on returning reported that the infantry were staying put, with no intention of moving in support, so he went back himself, spoke with the Commanding Officer of the unit, and returned with 60 infantrymen, taking them to support his Lewis gun lines and to dig-in. He then camouflaged his tank, placed five rifle-bombers inside to hold it as a strongpoint in its own right, called his crew together and then made his way back with them to St. Julien.

Thus ended one of the most successful combined-forces actions in the Great War – an action, meeting all its objectives, which could be said to be the saving grace of the tank as an arm for consideration by those in military power at the time.

It would not be too fanciful to claim that what happened at St. Julien on 19 August 1917, probably changed the face of modern warfare for all time. The brilliant first time fusion of tank and infantry resulted in a resounding success and opened many previously critical military eyes to the potential of the Tank. The road to Poelcappelle was opened, and the previously unconquerable enemy redoubts had fallen, at a cost of two killed and a couple of dozen wounded. This little action had been remarkable and a new dimension had entered the field of battle. This joining of the two arms, mechanical and infantry, had revised basic military thinking, but the lessons learned took a long time to sink in, and the astounding result of this action did nothing but cause further disasters for the tanks in the Ypres Salient. There were those who took it for granted that if such an action could succeed once, then it could be repeated frequently. Consequently, without thought for conditions and objectives, this type of approach was repeated frequently but, sadly, the successes weren't.

It must be said the Germans took on board most of the lessons learned, and they were to utilise them to good effect in another war twenty-five years later. It was the British casualty return of the Cockcroft operation that would convince them that there was something here worthy of study. The breathtaking early successes at the Battle of Cambrai later in the year would only underline those convictions. They developed their own machines and would put them to use in an even more compelling way across Europe in another war to be fought in the near future. The British, as is so often the case, invent, develop, use, but then let the strength of their concepts fall drastically behind, as they did with tanks during the post-war years.

Only in the Libyan desert campaigns of 1942-1943, and the brutal tank battles around the deadly 'bocage' countryside in Normandy in 1944, would the British revive their fortunes, and generally hone and polish their tank weapon until it was able to play its full part in the crushing Allied drive across Europe.

If they had developed the tank and its tactical use after 1917, and taken on board all the lessons so clearly to be learned, especially those around the Flemish crossroads at St.. Julien in 1917, who can tell what might have happened in the pre-1944 years of the Second World War.

The 'German's-eye-view' illustration of the action at St. Julien on the page following is a good example of how the British public were kept in touch with what was going on in the front line during the Great War.

Appearing in a popular London magazine on 1 September 1917, this over-dramatic interpretation of the action merited a full-page in the magazine, and was entitled:

"TANK v. FORTIN: Crushing a German Machine-Gun Stronghold"

and sub-titled:

"A trial of strength between our movable land-ships and the stationary concrete forts": A British Tank destroying a German Machine-gun fortress near St. Julien.

The caption to the illustration read:

One of the features in the German defensive systems in the Ypres salient was the fortress or fortified house. Owing to the "low visibility" many of these little forts escaped our heavy artillery preparation, and had to be attacked by the Tanks. In the incident here illustrated, a Tank came to the rescue of our infantry, and leisurely approaching the position, knocked out two machine-guns with a right and a left from its heavy sponson guns, and then walked over two more, bringing down a wall or two en route. The Tank's machine-guns then opened fire on the retreating garisson, causing heavy casualties. Writing on August 20 of recent Tank operations, Mr. Perry Robinson said: "The ground taken, which was north and north-east of St. Julien, included a number of strong points ... Yesterday's operation was practically a trial of strength between our movable land-ships and the stationary concrete forts, and the latter were hopelessly outmatched.

The illustration was produced by A. Forester, from material supplied by an 'eye-witness'. The name of the person who wrote the caption, is

not known. His *"... a Tank came to the rescue of our infantry and leisurely approaching the position, knocked out two machine guns with a right and a left from its heavy sponson guns, and then walked over two more, bringing down a wall or two en route."* defies description.

Perhaps both the 'eye-witness' and the very enthusiastic caption writer should have consulted with the G Battalion tank commanders, the supporting British infantry and the German strongpoint garrisons who took part in the action, before committing themselves to publishing such a work.

Notes:

1. Lieutenant E. T. Morgan and Second-Lieutenants H. G. Coutts and. A. G. Baker received an immediate award of the Military Cross after the action.

2. All five of the concrete-structured strongpoints that were the objectives in the Cockcroft operation were dismantled in the immediate years following the Armistice. The Belgian authorities in the 1920s halted the destruction of so many historic edifices, but the strongpoints so successfully taken in the St. Julien action were gone by then. Pond Farm, Cheddar Villa, Gourmier Farm and a few unnamed examples of German concrete redoubts along the old Wieltje line are the only ones left to be seen in this area. Alberta, a massive two-tiered strongpoint which stood slightly south-west of St. Julien, was there to see until the late 1960s, but, like so many others, it somehow slipped by the 1920 directive and, when last seen, was a pile of debris and rubble in the corner of a field. The original farms that were the base structure for these concrete redoubts have all been rebuilt on, or near, their original positions, but new buildings and road configurations make it fairly complicated to follow the attack, other than the first part where the road still veers left north of the starting point, before it takes its course between Hillock Farm and the farm track leading to the Gun Pit site

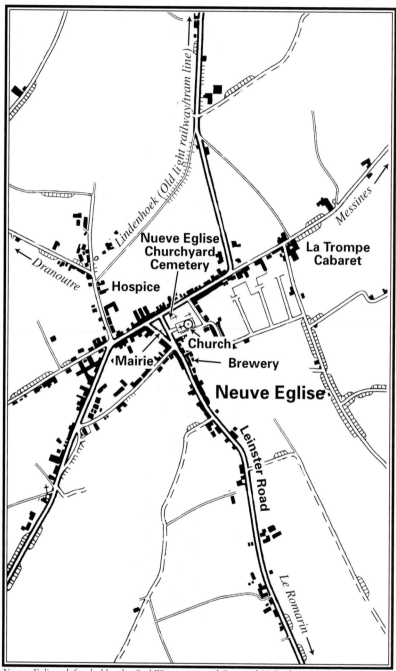

Lindenhoek (Old light railway/tram line)

Messines

Dranoutre

Nueve Eglise Churchyard Cemetery

La Trompe Cabaret

Hospice

Church

Mairie

Brewery

Neuve Eglise

Leinster Road

Le Romarin

Neuve Eglise, defended by the 2nd Worcesters and Corporal McBride in 1918

Yet all shall be forgot,
But he'll remember with advantages
What feats he did that day.
Shakespeare – Henry V.

9
CORPORAL MCBRIDE AND THE WORCESTERS AT NEUVE EGLISE
"B" Company, 33rd Battalion Machine Gun Corps,
and the 2nd Battalion the Worcestershire Regiment, April 1918.

FOLLOWING THEIR SUCCESSES along the River Somme in March 1918, having driven the British 5th Army back to the gates of Amiens, German High Command turned its attention to Flanders. Here they hoped to reap havoc of the same sort and break the British defences of Ypres, thus opening the way to the French coast from where they would take control of the English Channel, thereby determining the direction of British involvement in the war.

They had set-off alarm-bells throughout British High Command Headquarters as they attempted to capitalise on their crossing of the River Lys west of Armentières in the April of that year. The Messines Ridge, desperately defended and so bitterly fought over the year before, had fallen to them and, even worse, Mont Kemmel, so close to the French border, was lost in a disastrous week for the Allies. The British had handed over this strategically important position to the French, only to see it fall to a fast moving enemy.

The Germans now set their sights on the industrial plains of northern France behind the main British positions. To them, the towns of Bailleul and Hazebrouck, were mere hurdles on an obstacle course which, once they had been overcome, would leave a clear path to the ultimate prize.

The British position was desperate as the Germans flooded over the Flanders hills toward the French border with Bailleul already taking the brunt of their heavy shell-fire, a rare experience for this British Headquarter base town. The British infantry were fighting minor but furious rear-guard actions all along the line in a desperate bid to impede the seemingly unstoppable enemy advance.

Neuve Eglise, a small straggling village with its Mairie, church and market-square, perched on the high ground east of Bailleul, saw one such action. It lay in the path of the retreating British and advancing

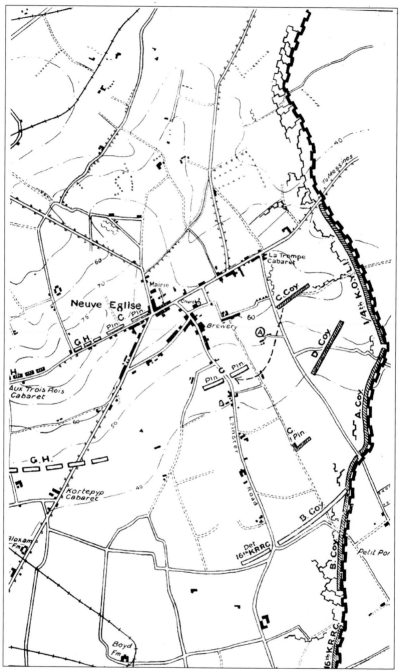

The Army Line and formations east of Neuve Eglise in April 1918

German armies and was about to achieve the distinction of becoming a battle honour on the colours of the 100th Machine Gun Company, then serving with the British 33rd Division.

Commanded by Lieutenant-Colonel Seton Hutchison, this unit had fought many fierce close-combat duels in the retreat. It was during one of these many rearguard actions that it formed a vital defensive position on the Hoegenmacher Windmill Hill just west of Bailleul. From 13 to 18 April, the battalion, less it's "B" Company, was instrumental in setting-up and holding a defensive line along this ridge, decimating the German onrush across the flat meadowlands towards Hazebrouck with murderously orchestrated machine-gun fire. This took the steam out of the enemy advance in this sector and it was here he was to incur his heaviest casualties.[1] These losses at the Hoegenmacher position during those five days caused one German source to state: *"The British had exacted some part revenge for their experience on the Somme in 1916".*

The time gained enabled the 1st Australian Battalion, Machine Gun Corps to be moved north to bolster the line in front of Hazebrouck at the Forest of Nieppe, on the night of 17-18 April – and the Germans were to advance no further. The line was held.

During this period the battalion's B Company, commanded by Major Lomax, was involved in an action of its own while attached to the 125th Division. On 12 April units of the division moved to occupy the half-completed Army Line reserve trenches running down from Neuve Eglise to northwest of Le Romarin, the sector covering the approaches to Bailleul. The 16th Battalion King's Royal Rifle Corps were positioned on the right of this line, with the 2nd Battalion Worcestershire Regiment holding the left, on the eastern fringes of the village of Neuve Eglise. Three machine gun sections of the 33rd Battalion's B Company were positioned in the forward zone outside Neuve Eglise, one section covering the approaches to the Ravelsburg Heights. The defending battalions watched the enemy advancing down the southern slopes of the Messines Ridge and on past Ploegsteert Wood, witnessing German field artillery galloping into a position out of range of the British musketry, setting up their guns and, over open sights, bombarding Neuve Eglise, reducing it to a heap of bricks and rubble.

On the morning of the 13th, the enemy infantry attacked in force. The companies of the 2nd Worcesters engaged to their front manning the Army Line, were unaware that another enemy force was advancing

The Worcestershires' Brewery headquarters in ruins, 1918

The Brewery site today

to their rear up Leinster Road from Le Romarin and Rue de Sac, driving-in the 16th K.R.R.C. on their right, and opening a large gap. They were moving close to the Worcesters' headquarters, located in the local brewery when the alarm was given. Lieutenant-Colonel Stoney, the commanding officer, led his men out of the headquarters to the cross-roads west of the church and held back the advance. His C company moved in behind the approaching German troops, penned them in the sunken road and literally slaughtered them. When they had finished the sunken road was heaped with dead Germans

Nevertheless the Worcesters' position was untenable and at 2 o'clock Lieutenant-Colonel Stoney decided to move his companies from the Army Line to the outskirts of the village itself. Enemy attacks continued throughout the afternoon and orders to withdraw were not able to be sent to his Army Line companies until 6 o'clock that evening.

This action had laid open the right flank of the Worcesters. With the enemy now filtering into the village, Stoney removed his Battalion Headquarters to the Hospice sited on the rising ground behind the village square, with the Germans in hot pursuit.

In this action the Machine Gun Corps' B Company had two men killed and two gun teams, with their guns, taken prisoner. Its two other teams, under Corporals J. Gilbert and P. McBride were positioned farther up the hill towards Neuve Eglise. Corporal Gilbert's team was captured in the hand-to-hand fighting taking place in the streets around the village, but McBride's team, retaliating with ferocious fire, pinned-down the enemy for a time. At this moment, McBride found himself the pivot of two backward movements, with the 16th K.R.R.C. retiring to his right and the 2nd Worcesters moving back into Neuve Eglise to his left. He deliberately exposed his team's rear to the enemy by swinging his gun through its traverse in order to stem the tide of the advancing enemy to his left, taking pressure off the retreating Worcesters.

Fierce and confused fighting lasted all morning on the slopes south of Neuve Eglise, with attack after enemy attack being beaten off throughout the afternoon. McBride's team, now comprising only himself and Privates J. Maulkin and A. Cator, spent the rest of the day, defending themselves against frequent, rapidly mounted raids. They then spent the whole of the night, without escort of any kind, fighting-off enemy patrols, not knowing what was on their flanks or to their rear. Dawn broke and they found themselves almost surrounded by the enemy. They quickly collected their gun, tripod and belt boxes and

The Neuve Eglise village square and Mairie, pre-1914

The Neuve Eglise village square and Mairie today

beat a hasty retreat, joining up with the Worcesters who by now were dispersed throughout the village.

In the morning attack the Worcesters had found themselves cut-off on both flanks, with no support or communication to their rear. Vicious hand-to-hand fighting took place in the streets in and around the now battered ruins of Neuve Eglise, particularly so in front of the village church and in the square housing its Mairie. Their headquarters, in a brewery just south of the church, was under threat and was forced to take up a new position in a Hospice north of the village crossroads on the Dranoutre road.[2] This operation was carried-out at 6.30 p.m. A section of Lieutenant-Colonel Stoney's report in the Worcestershire Battalion Diaries reads:

At 6.30 p.m., I moved Battalion H.Qs. to the MAIRIE *(sic)* and at once decided to hold it as a strong point, and issued instructions for its defence as follows:-

2 platoons were to be held as final reserve in the cellars.

1 platoon in addition to H.Q personnel were to defend the building.

1 platoon to occupy the house marked P.

Lewis Guns were to be placed in position on the ground floor behind windows and to cover the ground E. of the MAIRIE *(sic)* and also the main roads of the village and Church area.

3 riflemen were to man each window.

A M.G. which had just reported to me, was ordered to assist the Lewis

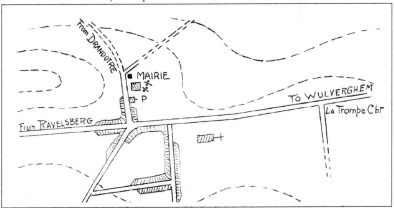

A map from the Worcestershire Battalion diaries showing the Hospice incorrectly identified as the Mairie, and the position of "the house marked P." referred to in the above extract from the diaries

The Neuve Eglise Hospice, pre-1914

The Neuve Eglise Hospice today, now a school's holiday home

Guns.

The platoon allotted to the house marked P. was to hold the road and generally act as a buffer to the MAIRIE *(sic)*.

The 'M.G'. mentioned was Corporal McBride and his two Privates.

Gradually the German advance forced the British line back astride the Wulverghem Road, causing the village square and the Hospice, with its battalion headquarters, to become the front line.

The three forward companies of the Worcesters had fallen back as ordered after dark on 13th April but, under non-stop pressure, most were forced to surrender, but many individual parties managed to leave the village to return to the remnants of the battalion.

What remained of D company held the enemy advance until its ammunition was exhausted, then withdrew in small groups to the Trompe Cabaret, a building on the Neuve Eglise–Messines road between the second line of defence west of the Army Line. Its commanding officer, Lieutenant C. S. Jagger organised the defence of this point until reinforcements arrived, then while withdrawing his detachment to rejoin the battalion, he was severely wounded. He was awarded the Military Cross for his work during this action and later, after the Armistice, went on to become a renowned sculptor, the creator of the Royal Artillery Memorial at Hyde Park Corner and the fresco *The Rampart,* now in the National Gallery, plus many other memorable pieces.

The Worcesters, having set up their defences before the Hospice, were under sustained attack throughout the whole evening, and both sides continued to lay down heavy machine gun and rifle fire throughout the night. Dawn of the 14th saw the Hospice, now housing Corporal McBride and his gun team and the Worcesters' Battalion Headquarters, completely surrounded and taking heavy trench mortar bombardment plus machine-gun fire from enemy teams on three sides. McBride, set up his gun in the top windows of the Hospice, and with the untiring support of Privates Maulkin and Cator, stemmed repeated rushes up the streets and across the village square, his withering machine-gun fire taking murderous effect on the German infantry, with the square and the church surrounds piled high with their corpses.

The garrison fought desperately, causing the enemy riflemen to withdraw, but machine guns still firing at the Hospice from three sides, supported by mortar and artillery fire, was causing casualties within. About 11 a.m., Assistant-Adjutant Captain J. Crowe volunteered to lead

The Hospice's position in relationship to the village sqauare, the photograph taken from the top of the Mairie.

a sortie against two machine guns sited on the high ground west of the Hospice to help clear a path for retreat.[3] This he did successfully and held the ground until, at 1.45 p.m., Lieutenant-Colonel Stoney, gave the orders to retire and the garrison left the Hospice, covered by Captain Crowe's captured machine guns and fire from the Hospice windows. This group of tired, battered men, 20 to 30 of them wounded, made its way onto the Dranoutre road and up to the comparative safety of Locre, leaving behind in the Hospice cellars, three men who were too badly wounded to be moved. The 33rd Battalion History records:

That day saw some of the bitterest hand-to-hand ever known to British soldiers. It is impossible to describe how men fought every inch of the retreat pressed back by continual fresh forces and overwhelming numbers. Many gallant sorties were made by the Worcestershires, led by the Assistant-Adjutant, who was awarded the V.C. for his conduct.

During this frantic and confusing period, Corporal McBride was never out of action. When his gun was destroyed he found another and put it into devastating action from the Hospice window. When German bombers attempted to rush the Hospice and bomb the occupants out of it, the corporal, now with rifle in hand, fired from the doorway, shooting the arms of the assaulting troops, exploding their bombs, whilst his team fired rifle grenades at point-blank range over the garden wall of the Hospice. He, with Privates Maulkin and Cator and the Worcesters' Battalion headquarter staff, were the last British troops to leave Neuve Eglise as the enemy moved in to occupy it.

Corporal McBride and Privates Maulkin and Cator, together with the remainder of the B Company gun sections under Major Lomax, who they had linked-up with after the retirement from the Hospice, rejoined the 33rd Battalion in its concentration area on the night of 18-19 April just before its withdrawal to Cassel. From there the Battalion moved to the Nordepeene area for a week of rest and recuperation.

Thus ended the action at Neuve Eglise for the 100th Infantry Brigade and what was left of B Company, 33rd Battalion, Machine Gun Corps

Corporal McBride was awarded the D.C.M and Private Maulkin the Military Medal for the parts they played in and around Neuve Eglise during those fateful days in April 1918. Today, Neuve Eglise has little to show of the role it was forced to play in the German offensive of April 1918. The village is very different today, although described by W. J. Bird in his *Thirteen Years After* as:

The view of the church from the Hospice garden today. The roof of the Mairie is visible behind the rooftops to the right of the picture. From the first floor of the Hospice, and with the houses in ruins, Corporal McBride would have a clear sight of these two buildings and the village square between them

Today, a granite base of a cross on one of the graves in the churchyard at Neuve Eglise bears witness to the action around the church in 1918

...... a village of some size ... the sidewalks were the worst I have seen in Belgium, a succession of mud holes and stones, with kitchen drains having openings on them in different places. The church is imposing, with its cemetery and memorial, but at one corner there is a small plot of white stones, a soldier's cemetery,

Typical of many of those that featured prominently in the period of the Great War, it is quiet, peaceful and prosperous, with little left, apart from its British Military cemetery and some bullet-scarred headstones in the churchyard cemetery, to remind the visitor of the part it played. Nevertheless, for those choosing to research the actions of 1918, the Neuve Eglise 'affair' is very easy to follow. The approaches to the village from the old Army Line have suffered little with re-building. The Brewery headquarters was rebuilt as a residential house, the church, Mairie, village square and Hospice are standing on their original sites and the street configuration has changed little. Houses mask the church and the square from the gardens of what once was the Hospice, but the church tower and the Mairie roof are clearly visible from it. The view that faced Corporal McBride and the 2nd Worcesters from the gardens of the Hospice, apart from these houses not now being bricks and rubble, and the church tower being intact, is much the same as it was in 1918. The elevation afforded from the top windows of the Hospice better give the gun-sight view that McBride 'enjoyed' during his short, but memorable, stay there. Captain Crowe's route against the German machine guns is easy to follow – and all this in a quiet country village well off the beaten-track for many battlefield coach tours.

Notes.

1. Lieutenant-Colonel Seton Hutchison, M.C., was awarded the D.S.O. for his defence of Hoegenmacher Windmill Hill in April 1918.

2. The building described in the 100th Machine Gun and the Worcestershire Regiment histories and battalion diaries as the Mairie, was in fact a Hospice which was completely destroyed during the war and rebuilt on its original site in the post war years. It was a Hospice until well after the second world war, but is now used as a school's holiday home. "The house marked P." used by the Worcestershires as an advanced post, a school house, was also destroyed and rebuilt. It now houses the local fire station. The Mairie, likewise made a total ruin by the actions of the war, was re-built in 1933 on its original site in the market square.

3. Assistant-Adjutant Captain J. Crowe was awarded the Victoria Cross and Second Lieutenant Pointon the Military Cross for this exploit.

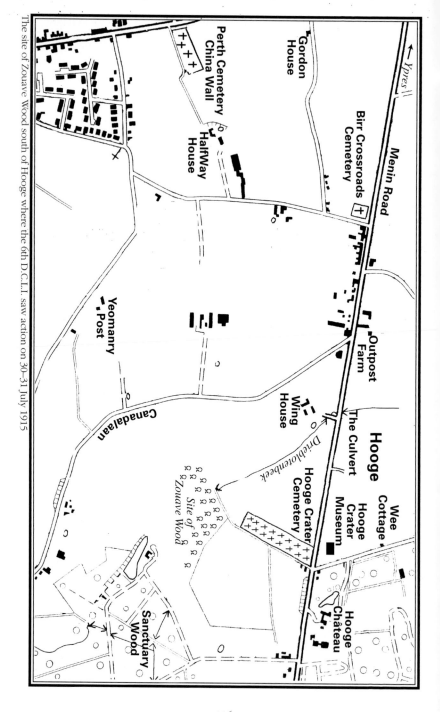

The site of Zouave Wood south of Hooge where the 6th D.C.L.I. saw action on 30–31 July 1915

Thou in our wonder and astonishment
Has built thyself a live-long monument,
And so sepulchred, in such pomp dost lie,
That Kings for such a Tomb would wish to die.
Wordsworth - Epitaph on Shakespeare.

10

TRIUMPH AND TRAGEDY

6th (Service) Battalion Duke of Cornwall's Light Infantry
Ypres Sector, June - August 1915

BEFORE THE OUTBREAK OF WAR in August 1914, Military High Command knew it would need to greatly increase its complements in all arms of the British Military Forces, and would need to do so soon after its Expeditionary Force mobilised for war. The necessary proposals were put forward to, and approved by, the Government of the time and, on 5 August 1914, The House of Commons authorised an expansion of the British Army by 500,000 men.

On the 7th, Lord Kitchener made his famous call for the first 100,000 men to form six divisions of the 'New Army' – the 9th to 15th Divisions – and within days he had his 100,000, plus many thousand more, and the authorities found themselves overwhelmed with men flooding to join the colours.

With no uniforms, equipment or accommodation to meet this unprecedented demand, the enlistment programme was called to a halt until such time as organisations were restructured to cope, and adequate supplies were made available. This soon happened and, very quickly all over the country, men were beginning to experience the disciplines and training necessary to knock them into the shape demanded of them by the regiments they were to join. All types of weaponry and uniforms were found to equip these new recruits to an army at war. Nevertheless, these New Army battalions of 'Kitchener's Men', the 'Service' battalions, or 'K' battalions as they were called, were soon trained up to the standard expected of them by the British Army.

They were formed from the very cream of the male civilian population of the country and enjoyed the great advantage of being superbly officered. Most of these officers were selected from the 500 Regular and Indian Army Officers home on leave at the outbreak of war. They were detained and posted to lead the mass of new men now forming part of the new British Army. Others were taken from the

Reserve of Officers, retired, wounded and convalescing officers, the Public School Officer Training Corps and, to support this solid base of leadership, authorisation was given to re-enlist the mass of ex-non-commissioned officers always to be found in Britain's civilian population. Within months, the Regular Army, together with its territorial support, now had the necessary battalions to form its extra divisions, all fit, trained and ready for war. The 'Kitchener' battalions were ready, officers and men alike, brimming with enthusiasm and keen to show their worth to their respective regiment's regular battalions.

One famous regiment of the Regular Army, the Duke of Cornwall's Light Infantry, the D.C.L.I., comprised at the declaration of war, five battalions – two regular, one militia and two territorial.

The 1st mobilised and left for France with the 5th Division, British Expeditionary Force; the 2nd prepared for war at its then current posting in Hong Kong and the 3rd was designated as a draft-funding unit, to 'feed' reinforcements to the active battalions. The 4th and 5th, the territorial battalions, took up war stations in Falmouth on the south coast of England. As territorials were not forced to serve overseas, a further battalion, the 4th Foreign Service Battalion, was made up from volunteers of the 4th and 5th to support the regulars on active service.

The Regiment added a sixth in 1914, its first 'K' battalion, the 6th (Service) Battalion. Formed at Aldershot on 14 September 1914, it went into training immediately and, in May of 1915, an eager, well-trained and highly disciplined battalion commanded by Lieutenant-Colonel T. R. Stokoe, left for France, keen to prove its worth to its regular 1st Battalion, already blooded and hardened in a war that was supposed to have been all over by Christmas, five months before.

It disembarked at Boulogne on 22 May as part of the 43rd Infantry Brigade, 14th (Light) Division, a division made up entirely of 'K' Battalions. Brigaded with the 6th Somerset Light Infantry, the 6th King's Own Yorkshire Light Infantry and the 10th Durham Light Infantry, it moved to the Bailleul area at the end of the month before moving on to billets at La Clytte. On arrival, its 'A' Company was immediately attached as trench-diggers and support troops to their 1st Battalion, already in the front line in the Zillebeke Switch trench system.

It was then attached to the 14th Infantry Brigade, working with its own 1st Battalion for instruction in trench warfare, two companies going to the front at a time. On 20 May the battalion moved into camp at Poperinghe from where, on the 24th, it took up positions in dugouts in the Ramparts at Ypres.

The 25 June saw the 43rd Brigade relieve its sister brigade, the 42nd in the trench lines east of Ypres, with the 6th D.C.L.I. staying in reserve in the town itself, supplying carrying parties for those in the front line trenches. On the 29th the Brigade was relieved and moved back to billets and bivouacs near Vlamertinghe where it stayed until, on 12 July, it was instructed to prepare to relieve the 42nd Brigade in the line on the night of 18th/19th of the month.

In its two months in Belgium the battalion had become accustomed to the type of trench warfare known only to those who served in the Ypres Salient, most of the time spent diving into dugouts dodging flying masonry and bricks caused by the bombardments of Ypres, or cowering against the walls of muddy trenches under incessant and terrifying enemy gunfire. The men had 'played themselves in' and had the confidence and belief that their battalion was as good as any in the line.

They needed this confidence when called to 'stand to' to support the 6th Division, then positioned on its left flank, in an attack on German trenches, adjacent to the little hamlet of Hooge on the Menin Road east of Ypres.

At 7.00 p.m. on the 19th a tremendous roar heralded the explosion of a mine by the 6th Division beneath an enclosed German work alongside Hooge. The explosion, taking the Germans by surprise, was the signal for the Cornwalls to open fire, covering men of the 6th Division's charge across No-Man's Land to occupy the crater, the crater that was to become the infamous Hooge Crater, which they did, and with few casualties.[1]

In retaliation a surprised and furious enemy swept the British trench lines all through the night of the 19th with guns of all calibres, including, for good measure, their deadly trench-mortars, the much feared *Minenwerfers*, and continued to do so throughout the following days of the 20th–26th. On the 24th, Lieutenant-Colonel Stokoe, the 6th Battalion's Commanding Officer, had been made a casualty by a trench-mortar bomb and, on the 26th, Second-Lieutenants Saxan and Harrison were both wounded with a number of other ranks by a large shell falling in the trenches.

After eight days of non-stop bombardment the weary men of the 6th were relieved with the rest of their Brigade by troops of the 42nd Brigade. They withdrew for a much needed and well-earned rest to a

German infantry learning to use their new weapon

camp west of Vlamertinghe having suffered casualties of four officers and 60 other ranks.[2] Four days later, at 4 a.m. on the 30th, rested and re-equipped, the battalion was ordered to 'stand to' as the enemy, using their terrifying new weapon, liquid fire, for the first time against British troops, had driven the front line companies of the Rifle Brigade from

two lines of trenches in front of Sanctuary and Zouave Woods, north and south of the Menin Road at Hooge. The 6th Battalion went straight into the line under the orders of the 41st Brigade to take part in a counter-attack to reclaim the lost trenches. 'A' and 'B' companies moved forward to the rear of Sanctuary Wood and 'C' and 'D' to the rear of Zouave Wood to support the attack. During the move Major J. J. P. Jones-Parry was killed and 30 other ranks were killed or wounded, a clear indication of the intensity of the German barrage, a veritable tornado of shells hammering and smashing through Zouave and Sanctuary Woods.

Major J. J. Jones-Parry

The counter-attack failed miserably with men of the 7th and 8th Battalions Rifle Brigade leaving the cover of the wood and advancing uphill toward an entrenched infantry supported by well-sited machine guns which played havoc with their depleted companies. The 6th D.C.L.I.'s 'C' and 'D' companies were ordered to advance into Zouave Wood, moving through these exhausted, battered and bruised riflemen, survivors of what must have been one of the most pointless, ill-prepared and wasteful counter-attacks of the Great War. An ineffective three-quarter of an hour's bombardment followed by an attack using troops of the decimated companies of battalions who had already suffered horrendous fighting that day was doomed to failure before it started. Counter-attacking upward toward well placed enemy weaponry which was covering the open ground with a hailstorm of rifle and machine-gun bullets as well as heavy mortar fire, they were cut down before they were able to reach their own wire. It took a full divisional attack well supported by heavy artillery bombardments nine days later to do what those handful of battle-worn, inexperienced troops were expected to do in a hastily planned counter-attack after a non-stop 12-hour hammering by artillery, Minenwerfers, liquid fire, machine guns and rifle-fire.

The attack Companies of the 6th D.C.L.I. advanced into their positions, manning the lines flanking either side of the wood, known as

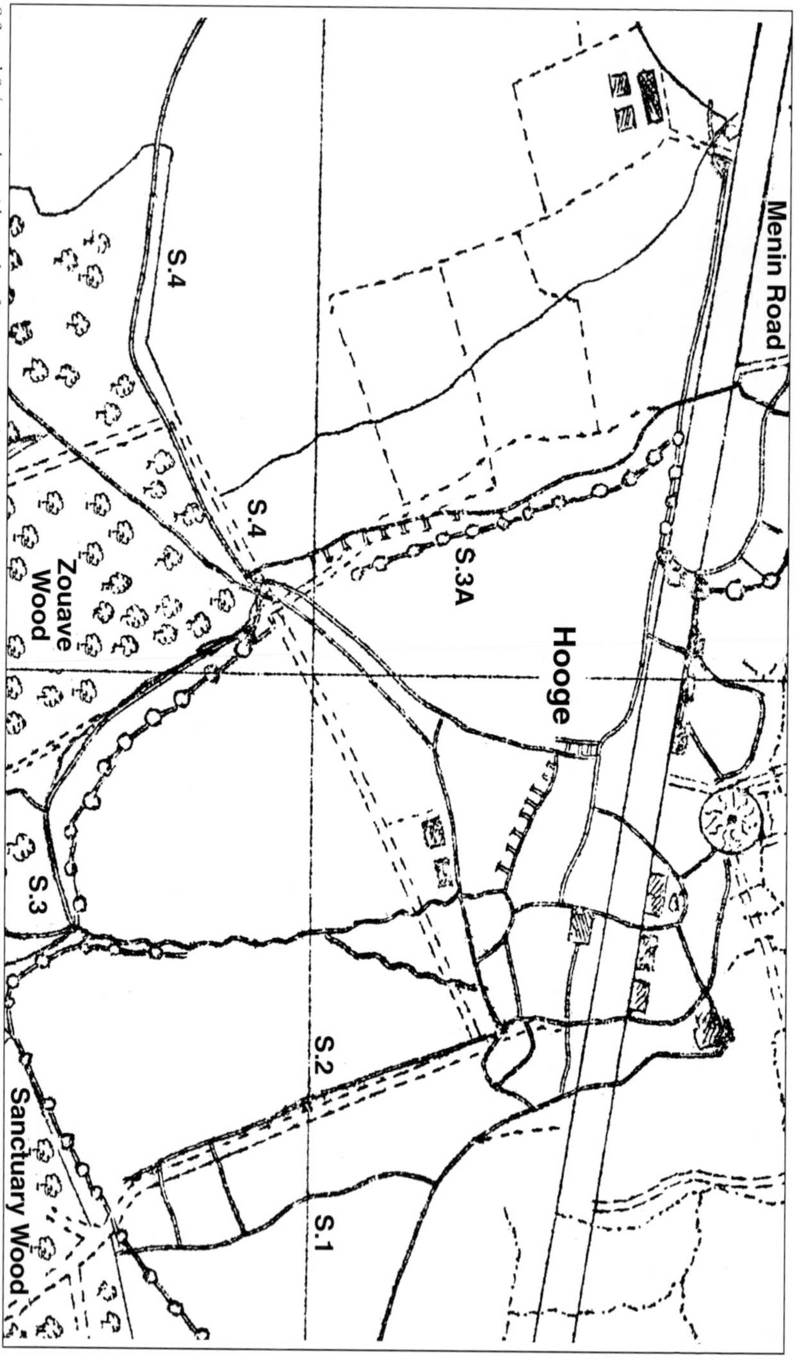

S.3 and S.4 trenches either side of Zouave Wood, the positions held by companies of the 6th Battalion D.C.L.I

Menin Road

Hooge

Zouave Wood

Sanctuary Wood

S.4

S.4

S.3A

S.3

S.2

S.1

S.3 and S.4, where their 'A' and 'B' companies joined them from behind Sanctuary Wood. Still under heavy bombardment, all four companies took heavy casualties during their forward movement.

At 7.00 p.m., preceded by heavy bombardment, the German infantry attacked, with, amongst its numbers, specially trained troops with liquid fire equipment strapped to their backs Some of the men of 'C' Company, having lost all their officers and N.C.O.'s broke about 30 yards of front and began to fall back. Their own machine-gunners, just in the rear, threatened to open fire on them if they did not return to their positions, yelling at them that the 6th Cornwalls were going to "bloody well stick it". The men of 'C' Company quickly returned to their positions in the line where, supported by heavy artillery, they helped beat-off the attack, the Germans fleeing back across No-Man's Land taking heavy casualties from the Cornwalls' accurate rifle and machine-gun fire. All through the night of the 30th, the battalion clung to its trenches under extremely heavy artillery and trench mortar fire. By daybreak it had lost three of its officers killed, including the medical officer, two officers wounded and about 100 other ranks killed or wounded. Again, throughout the 31st, the battalion held the line suffering tremendous artillery fire laid down from the south, east and the north of its positions, literally saturating its trenches. At midnight the Germans attacked again but, as before, the D.C.L.I. drove them back, desperately holding its line under a hailstorm of British and German shells shrieking through the air, as the artillery of both sides took it out on each other in a round of desperate duels. Nothing would move the Cornwalls, but once more they paid a price in casualties – three officers killed, two wounded and 80 more other ranks killed or wounded. Relief came at last when at 1.00 a.m., a sister battalion of the 14th Division, the 6th Battalion King's Own Yorkshire Light Infantry, filed into their trenches, taking over this shell-battered, devastated part of the line.

The Battalion retired to the Ramparts at Ypres, depleted in strength, battle-scarred and exhausted, with only seven of its officers left, but it was a 'K' Battalion with a triumphant story to tell. It had held its line in Zouave Wood against all odds. It had withstood all that the German artillery and trench mortar companies could offer and had beaten-off several attacks by a determined infantry. The enemy it faced had held the advantage of positions on high ground, commanding observation and a field of fire over the Cornwall's line for about 300 yards. An impossible situation, but the 6th had held its line, not ceding one yard

The area of the 6th Battalion's action at Zouave Wood today. The distinct shape of the never-replanted site of Zouave Wood is easily recognisable by the triangled shape of ploughed land south of Hooge Crater Cemetery of ground, while taking casualties of seven officers killed and wounded and 285 other ranks killed or wounded. Since marching from Vlamertinghe two days before, this new breed of soldier, these 'civvies in khaki', had shown their worth under 36 hours of appalling, non-stop shell- and rifle-fire inter-dispersed with the added terror accompanying Germany's latest contribution to warfare, liquid fire. Adding to their discomfort, these weary, battle-worn troops had had nothing to eat or drink for 48 hours.

29-year old Sergeant Major Frederick Hillersdon Keeling, later killed in action in France on 18 August 1916, left, in a letter home, the following account of his own part in the 6th Battalion's action:

I have been in the battle - I think it is pretty well a battle - which you will read about in the papers, and I am wounded, but not badly. We stood to in our rest camp at 4.30 this morning. The big guns had been going some time. We marched about three or four miles and then halted. The news came of the German attack with liquid fire. Then another brigade of our Division sent to ask our regiment for bombers to detonate - that is, to prepare for exploding - three or four hundred bombs. I took three of my four sections up to their Brigade Headquarters and did the job. At first they proposed to send us as a separate detachment to the

firing-line to replace the bombers of a regiment which had suffered badly, but the Major commanding now, as our Colonel was wounded in the trenches last week, wanted to keep us, so we rejoined our battalion about 11.45 finding our way to a given point on the map. Then we went up to supports and were shelled heavily all the way up. One company officer was killed and several men wounded. At 2 p.m. our batteries started giving them hell. They replied. We were near the firing line then and things were warm, but the great thing to keep you cool and happy is to have something to do. I could never have lived through the nine days in the trenches last time if I

Sergeant Major Frederick H. Keeling,

had not been worked to death day and night. We waited in a support trench half an hour. My bombers had got mixed up with the company's, but there were enough to make a unit. I was ordered to lead the second party which went up to support the firing-line. I led my men across a field which had been heavily shelled just before, but fortunately we got none. We reported to the 8th Rifle Brigade C.O. in the wood; he sent us on to the right; shells were falling everywhere. I passed several men dead or horribly wounded; less wounded men were wending their way back to the dressing station. I felt cheerful nevertheless, really a sort of tinge of joy of battle in spite of the hellishness of it all, though you can't get a real joy of battle in these artillery days. Then suddenly I heard a specially loud crash and fell, seeing "red", and thinking, "Am I going to die? This is not so bad as I thought it would be; let me get the thing tied up before I suffer from loss of blood," which I could feel and see a good deal of.

As I rushed to an officer and asked him to do me up I thought, "What a coward I am, not looking to my corporal!" who was wounded next to me. However, there was no arterial bleeding - I learnt about this at our M.O.'s lectures on First Aid. I had got about four cuts on the back of the head and neck, and slight cuts on ear and hand, and various bruises on legs and arms. The officer did me up and I reminded him of the iodine, which he forgot at first. Then I cam back to the dressing station a little ashamed of not going back to the firing-line. It was awfully difficult to say whether one was bad enough not to go back; however, they all said I must not go back, so I came here. It isn't a Blighty I am pretty sure, so shan't see you yet, and shall be back to have another smack at them with Ticklers' Artillery soon. I am not sure whether it was a shell itself or whether a shell fragment hit one of the bundles of bombs we were carrying up and exploded them. The only trouble now is if one will get down all right. The shelling has died away a bit now, though they are still exploding uncomfortably near this dugout. There are contrary rumours as to whether we have taken the lost trenches or not - the ones we took from the Germans about the middle of June and lost a week ago - anyhow, if I post this letter you will know I am alright - I have suffered no pain really.

The same evening from the dressing station he continued:

Have been dressed properly and expect to go off to the casualty clearing station in a few hours and meanwhile I will try and get a 'kip'. I have had a very lucky escape and I feel I have done some good work to-day. They ran short of bombs last night. I got 350 up to them and although at least ten out of my fifty-five bombers were knocked-out by 5 p.m. and I never chucked one bomb myself, I have left some good men up there who will do fine work when required.[3]

The battalion were to enjoy three days of comparative rest in the Ypres Ramparts before, on 5 August, being detailed for trench supply carrying parties for a few hours. They were then relieved by the Queen's Westminster Rifles and marched-off to dugouts on the Vlamertinghe Road, just west of Ypres, and from there into bivouacs just northwest of Vlamertinghe itself. A few more days of rest then, on 9 August, they were called to 'stand to' again while the 6th Division launched an attack on Hooge, re-capturing all that had been lost during that devastating period on 30 to 31 July, and taking 400 yards of the enemy's trenches north of the Menin Road while they were at it.

On the 10th, the battalion marched back to Ypres and took up billets in the many cellars there. Battalion Headquarters plus 100 men established themselves in the cellars of the Ecole Mayenne opposite the old Belgian Infantry Barracks, 150 men were billeted in the cellars at the nearby St. Josef Convent in the same street, while the rest of the battalion found their billets in the St. Martin's Cloisters in the southern wing of the Cathedral and in the vast cellars of the Cloth Hall and the Notre Dame Hospital in the town square.

Ypres, as usual was taking its usual amount of enemy shelling but it was noticed that enemy aircraft were particularly active on the 11th, then, at about 6.30 on the morning of the 12th, German artillery opened a very heavy bombardment on Ypres, targeting the Town Square and St. Martin's Cathedral with 17-inch shells intermingled with smaller calibre and shrapnel shells. The 17-inch gun was known to be that nicknamed "the Ypres Express", firing from Houthulst Forest, roughly ten miles away, but there was confusion at the time as to whether it was searching for an observation post in the tower of St. Martin's Cathedral, or whether the move to the cellars by the battalion had been spotted by enemy aircraft the day before with the bombardment intended to cause as much havoc to it as was possible.

Whatever the case, the shelling soon brought down the ceiling of St. Martin's Cloisters burying a number of men of 'C' and 'D' companies who, thinking they were safe within the confines of the Cloisters, had made no effort to move. Many others, in attempting to rescue their comrades were themselves buried. Two officers, Major C. Barnett and Adjutant-Lieutenant R. C. Blagrove, rushing from Battalion Headquarters

The entrance to the cellars at Ypres where men of the 6th Battalion D.C.L.I were billeted.

to organise rescue attempts, were killed immediately by a shell, landing just north of the Cloisters. Orders were soon issued for everyone to keep well away from the shelled area but the Company Chaplain, a Mr Harris, insisted on going back to help in the rescue attempts aided by four volunteers from the battalion. He was severely wounded while striving to release some of the entrapped men, as was 'C' Company's Captain Andrews. Rescue work was quickly taken over by men of the fast-arriving 11th King's Liverpool (Pioneers) who worked through the whole of the afternoon, in spite of the continuous shelling. The end result for the 6th Cornwalls was five men rescued from the collapsing cellars, two officers killed, two wounded, nineteen other ranks killed and eighteen wounded. Major Barnett and Lieutenant Blagrove were buried in the prison near the Water Tower by the West Gate of Ypres together with the rest of the fatalities. They were later moved, during the concentration of graves in the 1920s, to a cemetery then called the "Cemetery North of the Prison" and later "Ypres Reservoir North Cemetery" which is today's Ypres Reservoir Cemetery.[4]

Sadly, this was not the full extent of the out-of-the-line tragedy that befell the 6th Battalion as, during the clearing-up of the town after the Armistice, 40 bodies of its 'B' Company men were discovered in the cellars of the Cloth Hall. This discovery, together with the story of the men who died in St. Martin's Cloisters, have, with the passing of time, become intermingled and have led to the general belief that the line of 16 headstones in Plot V, Row AA, marking the graves of those buried in the Ypres Reservoir Cemetery are of those found after the Armistice, a belief supported by the cemetery register. A close inspection of the badly deteriorated headstones of those 16 men will show the wording "Believed to be", on each one of them, a sure sign that they had been buried during war, with their graves being lost in a later bombardment, They certainly were not buried after the Armistice.

Notes:

1. This Hooge Crater, the original, was in-filled due to the amount of corpses and debris therein and to the fact that it was considered untenable. The craters, three of them, now ornamental ponds, which are to be found in front of today's Hooge Château, rebuilt on the site of the original stables, are frequently referred to as the in-filled and infamous Hooge Crater which they are not.

2. A wounded Private W. Jones of the 6th (Service) Battalion Duke of Cornwalls Light Infantry was presented with the Distinguished Conduct Medal for conspicuous bravery on the night of June 28/29 during the course of this action

near Hooge. His was possibly the first won by the New Army.

3, Frederick Hillersdon Keeling, better known to his Cambridge contempories as 'Ben', was a leading and passionate member of the Fabian Society and friend of both Rupert Brooke and J. C. Squire. An instinctive socialist, he had an unhappy childhood and was orphaned at 17 whilst at Winchester. During his years at Trinity College, Cambridge he was befriended by H. G. Wells and became active in Cambridge Socialist circles. Taking up the post of assistant editor of the New Statesman he became particularly concerned with the welfare of child-workers and Local Authorities involvement. Once war was declared Frederick Keeling immediately joined the Artists Rifles with Rupert Brooke but refused any offer of a commission and by the end of August 1914 became a private in the 6th Battalion Duke of Cornwall's Light Infantry. A holder of the Military Medal, he was one of the many killed in action during the 6th Battalion's attack on Delville Wood on Friday 18 August 1916. Like many of those that fell in the Delville Wood action, his name is commemorated on the Thiepval Memorial to the Missing on the Somme.

4. Three cemeteries were started near the prison the reservoir and the Western Gate of the Ypres ramparts. Two between the prison and the reservoir were moved to the third, which was called the "Cemetery North of the Prison", later "Ypres Reservoir North Cemetery" and now, "Ypres Reservoir Cemetery"

The 16 headstones of men of the 6th D.C.L.I. who died in the bombardment of St. Martin's Cathedral in Ypres on 12th August 1915

The 'Believed to be' inscription which appears on each of the sixteen headstones in Plot V, Row AA in the Ypres Reservoir Cemetery

The site of The Birdcage at Ploegsteert Wood

'The most diabolical splendour I have ever seen.
Philip Gibbs - War Correspondent

11
THE FIVE FORGOTTEN MINES OF MESSINES
Ploegsteert Sector 1917 and 2000

URING THE GREAT WAR of 1914–1918, there were eight major battles launched between 31 July and 26 October 1917. Collectively called Third Ypres, but perhaps better known as the Battles for Passchendaele, they were preceded by a battle to clear the enemy from his strongly-fortified areas on the ridges running from Mount Sorrel, south-east of Ypres, past Wytschaete and Messines to the valley of the River Douve. From these high points the Germans commanded observation over the British lines below Ypres, giving them the ability to strike at the flank of any attack originating from within the Ypres Salient.

British High Command deemed it essential to eliminate this threat to ensure the successful launch of those major battles aimed at ousting the enemy from Flanders. Thus was conceived a deep-mine offensive that would later be called the Battle of Messines, a battle that, although seemingly unconnected, was an integral part of Third Ypres.

The idea of a mining offensive on the Second Army front dated from July 1915, but the proposal to develop it to a major offensive can be said to date from the September of that year. From that date, deep-mining was planned and progressed, resulting in twenty-four mines being tunnelled-in, mostly in pairs. under major German strongpoints from Hill 60, south of Zillebeke, to Le Pelerin on the eastern edge of Ploegsteert Wood. On the day, 7 June 1917, only nineteen were triggered, four being outside the battle areas finally chosen for the offensive and one below La Petite Douve Farm south of the village of Messines, being abandoned due to German counter-mining activity.

Official histories made mention of the number of mines laid, but leave room for doubt on their accuracy in that they all differ:

Brigadier-General Sir James E. Edmonds, C.B., C.M.G., *in The History of the Great War, Military Operations, France and Belgium 1917,*

Volume II, 7th June–10th November, gives detail as:

Only 2 mines, one at Petite Douve Farm and one at Kruisstraat were lost and 3 mines at the Birdcage were not fired. 19 were blown on 7th June.

Colonel H. Stewart, CMG, DSO, MC. in his *The Official History of New Zealand Division's Effort in the Great War, Vol II, France* states simply:

In all, twenty-four mines were constructed, four of which were outside the front ultimately selected for our offensive.

and Dr. C. E. W. Bean, in his *The Official History of Australia in the War of 1914-18, volume IV, The A.I.F. in France 1917,* implies that there were 27 mines laid:

By the date of the battle, twenty-three deep mines had been tunnelled beneath the German front line ... The British also had four mines ready charged beneath 'The Birdcage', 400 yards further south. It was at first intended to explode these also, but this decision was altered. If the mines were fired, the craters might be useful to the enemy, whereas if they were kept ready to fire they might greatly assist a later operation. In the end, owing to the subsequent German retirement, they were not fired.

The four mines tunnelled-in below The Birdcage 280 yards further south of the Factory Farm pair, the most southerly to be blown at the opening of the battle, were originally planned to fire with the rest but it was decided that the enemy, who had proved himself adept in the past at gaining an advantage from the British mining tactics, might do so again. In the vicinity of these mines, his reserves would be closer to the resulting craters than the British attack force and, by occupying the lips of the craters as had been his habit with previous mine explosions, would cause serious problems to the ranks of the oncoming infantry. It was therefore decided not to blow them, but to keep them, fully-charged, for use in later operations in the sector, maybe in the days following the battle-opening to extend the right flank. As it was they were never used, the enemy retirement from the Messines Ridge and its surrounds after the fighting closed causing them to be made surplus.

These four were driven-in by the 171st Tunnelling Company from two shafts opened in Trench 121 which ran due eastward from the northern tip of Ploegsteert Wood before meeting the Le Pelerin–St. Yves road where it made a sharp left turn following the edge of the road to link with Trench 122, which in turn linked with Trench 123, then on to

Trench 124, and so on, and so on, up the line in this sector.

The Birdcage, the site which they were intended to eliminate, was a sprawling mass of defensive trenches, dug-outs and barbed-wire entanglements located at Le Pelerin, a tiny community on the eastern edge of Ploegsteert Wood, an area that had been held by the Germans since October 1914. Originally part of the British line held by the 9th Lancers, 2nd Cavalry Brigade, 4th Division, it was overrun by the Germans during their unsuccessful attempt to break through the British lines from Le Gheer to St. Yves. They then fortified it to protect the approaches eastward towards Warneton and Comines. It was a small salient in its own right, pushing into the British line, almost to the edge of the wood just north of Le Gheer and the southern edge of St. Yves. It was so heavily wired, in many parts over 6-feet high, that it was nicknamed the Birdcage by an early British unit facing it, a name it kept for the rest of the war. It was one of those rare areas of the Western Front which never changed hands. Generally speaking this was a 'quiet' area of the front in Belgium and was used primarily by both belligerents as a sector to train and acclimatise their incoming units into the rudimentary art of trench warfare, although a great deal of small-mine activity by the British and frequent raiding from both sides kept the troops in this sector on their toes.[1].

The 7 June offensive was the high point of activity in the Ploegsteert sector for the remainder of 1917 and 1918, other than when the Germans occupied the wood briefly in the April of 1918. The responsibility for the mines under The Birdcage was taken over by the Belgian authorities with a view to them conducting surveys with the Tunnelling Companies to remove them at a later date, at a time when the pressure of work on these companies was less heavy. The mine positions were identified with concrete markers but, in 1918 when peace came and the work of reconstruction commenced, no further thought seemed to have been given to them. The charges, in their underground chambers, would possibly have remained dormant for all time, but for one of them being set-off during a particularly heavy thunderstorm in the summer of 1955, triggered by a bolt of lightning striking a nearby electricity pylon's stabilising hawser and pin.[2]

After 38 years of inactivity, 32,000 lbs of ammonal roared into life from 65 feet below, turning a large section of the land into a massive crater. Fortunately, there were no casualties and the local authorities quickly repaired the damage, returning this area to its quieter, more tranquil atmosphere, as befits an agricultural neighbourhood.

The mine had erupted in a field on the left-hand side of the road running from Le Pelerin toward La Basse-Ville, a small hamlet on the way to Warneton. This road, a turning off the one which skirts the eastern fringe of the wood, was the very road that dissected the old Birdcage, its eastern stretch being that which served as the main enemy supply route for troops and materials into it.

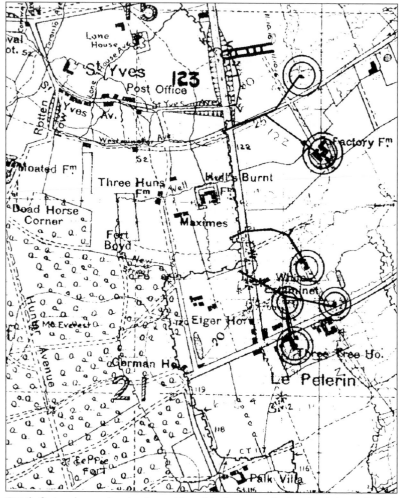

Detail of a trench map showing the position of the four unused mines in relation to the two blown at factory farm, the latter two being the most southerly exploded at the opening of the 7 June offensive in 1917

As with many of the destroyed dwellings in Belgium, post-war rebuilding took place on, or very near, the old footings of the original houses and farms, as was the case with Le Pelerin. Second and Third House (military mapmakers reference points) which, with one or two others, made up almost the entire housing community of this tiny hamlet, were rebuilt on their original sites. German House (sometimes called First House), a game-keeper's dwelling just within the wood, was completely destroyed and never rebuilt, its footings and brick-rubble, now covered in overgrowth, the only evidence of its ever being. An enemy sniper and observation post in the early days of the war, it was

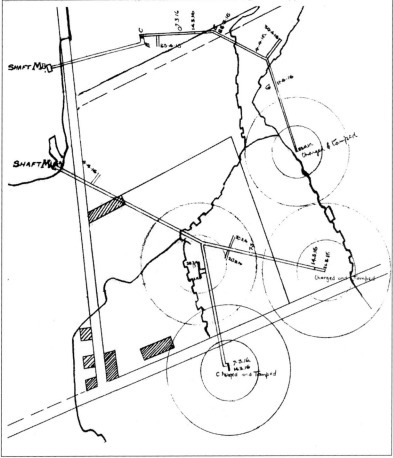

Diagram showing the two tunnels driven-in from Trench 121 and the chambers of the four unused mines below the Birdcage

the target of a raid by the 11th Infantry Brigade, 4th Division on 19 December 1914, which saw the death of the Captain the Honourable Richard George Grenville Morgan-Grenville of the 1st Battalion Rifle Brigade. He was carried back by his men and now lies buried with others who fell in the raid, in Rifle House Cemetery, within the wood.

Today the little hamlet of Le Pelerin, in keeping with similar ones throughout Belgium, boasts many more dwellings as population grows and the desire to live in buildings of a more modern style flourishes. The two Factory Farm craters slightly to the north of the Birdcage position, one in an open field surrounded by a light growth of trees and the other, surrounded by a heavier growth and used as a cattle watering source, is wired-off and hidden by its position on a high rise of ground, are the only evidence to suggest that anything like a war, or even a trench, ever traversed this quiet backwater on the Franco-Belgian border.

The site of this 1955 crater can be identified when the crop is down by a slight rise in the field caused by the in-fill. On the other side of the road further back toward the wood, a slight depression, with a light

The water-filled indent showing the position of the mine on the other side of the road to that which blew in 1955

growth on its surrounds, better seen in rainy weather, again when the crop is down and water has gathered on the surface, marks the spot of another of the four. This one sits 65-feet below the surface with 34,000 lbs worth of ammonal as its charge.

The other two are well-hidden below the same field across the road which held the first. Both of them about 400 feet from it, one due east containing 26,000 lbs of ammonal at 80 feet down, and the other, northwest of it at 70 feet below, containing 20,000 lbs of the charge. These two mine chambers would certainly have felt the underground impact from the 1955 explosion, and this impact may well have sealed their fate for all time, but who knows?

One of these four was mentioned in the Argyll and Sutherland Highlanders' war history in an account stating:

A tunnel was dug by the Tunnelling Company from our front-line to The Birdcage which was a system of trenches in the enemy's support line and so powerfully was it charged it was expected that no men in The Birdcage would escape. Our men used to carry up the ammonal at night in boxes which were popularly known by the men as 'Chocolate Boxes'. The secret of the mine was wonderfully kept and though we had a shrewd idea of what was going on not a word of it was mentioned. It is doubtful whether this mine was ever blown. Unkind people used to say that as soon as we placed the ammonal in the mine the Boche used to take it out from the other end!

The Germans certainly didn't take the ammonal out of the one that blew in 1955, although there will be some local residents that hope they managed such a feat with the other three, that is assuming that the local community are aware of what rests below the surface in the close-by fields.

Road traffic is never very heavy in this area, but that which does use the road in both directions from Le Pelerin to La Basse-Ville and Warneton might well consider another route if it were aware of what lies close-by, beneath the fields edging the wood and, likewise, the tractor-drivers working the fields might have second thoughts about the way they approached certain sections of them.

All the coach parties, motor car drivers and battlefield-walkers who visit the site of the old Birdcage, whilst enjoying the pleasant views of this peaceful rural area and its beautiful wood, might give a thought to what the Great War tunnellers, bravely and efficiently, placed and left below them over eighty years ago.

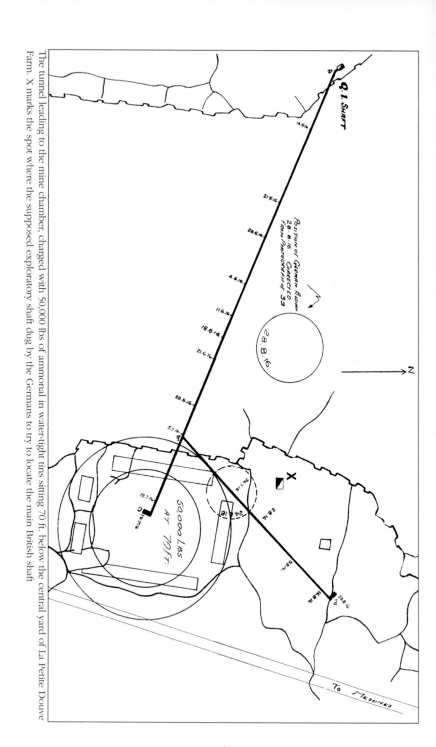

The tunnel leading to the mine chamber, charged with 50,000 lbs of ammonal in water-tight tins sitting 70 ft. below the central yard of La Petite Douve Farm. X marks the spot where the supposed exploratory shaft dug by the Germans to try to locate the main British shaft

140

So much for the four mines that were left un-triggered at the outset of the Battle of Messines in June 1917. But what of the one that was abandoned? The mine destined to blow La Petite Douve Farm into oblivion was tunnelled-in from Trench 135, initially by the 3rd Canadian Tunnelling Company but continued and finalised by the 171st Tunnelling Company. This one was eventually abandoned and its chamber flooded because the Germans were well aware of its existence and were conducting serious and damaging underground counter-mining attacks against it.

Because of the mine chamber's close proximity to the River Douve the charge, 50,000 lbs of ammonal placed 70ft below the central farmyard itself, was specially packed and protected in water-tight tins. Assuming the packaging of the ammonal was well done, and there is every reason to believe it was, as was just about everything else related to the Battle of Messines, then these water-tight tins are still sitting there, protecting their dangerous content and, maybe, waiting for a convenient lightning-strike to help them prove their worth, finishing the job destined for them early that morning of 7 June 1917.

A concrete slab just outside the farm complex covers a supposed exploratory shaft the Germans used in their attempt to locate the main British tunnel and galleries, but the main shaft, from which they blew in the galleries with camouflets, is located in the field adjacent to the farm, about 300 ft. due northwest of the centre of the yard and north of the British tunnel driven-in from Trench 135. The opening to this shaft recently collapsed and is now surrounded by a protective fence to ensure the safety of those animals and others using the field. The resident farmer obviously knows of the mine's existence, but does he know of the water-tight tins?

So the five forgotten mines of Messines are accounted-for. Prior to the information of the Le Pelerin four coming to light, it was generally believed that information relating to their actual position, apart from the one that blew in 1955, had been lost for all time. Whether or not the knowledge of their whereabouts will prove beneficial, particularly to those who live and work nearby, is questionable. Certainly future generations should be made aware of their existence as, if industrial development does spread to this part of Belgium, the heavy-duty excavating equipment of a construction company of that time may well do what British High Command chose not to do in 1917, but what a lightning-strike in 1955 effectively showed could be done.

Notes:

1. On 13 May 1916, the Germans targeted trenches around Moated Farm north of Ploegsteert Wood with a view to destroying a mine-shaft they believed to be there. Men of the 11th Battalion Royal Scots, 9th (Scottish) Division had spent much time in working-parties helping the tunnelling company to drive this mine to The Birdcage. The Germans, the 104th Saxons, attacked in three raiding-parties of twenty men each, following a violent barrage. The Royal Scots counter-attacked, and drove the Germans back, but lost sixteen killed, 61 wounded and eight missing. The Germans left behind ten dead in the Royal Scots' trenches. One man was to benefit well from this raid. Part of the trench-line that had taken a major part of the bombardment had resulted in all the men being killed except for one officer and a private who was serving a three-year sentence in the line for attempted desertion. During the raid he bayoneted and killed six Germans while the officer killed two with his revolver. The officer won the Military Cross and the private had his sentence quashed.

2. In their Cameos of the Western Front series of books, *Salient Points One* and *A Walk Round Plugstreet*, the authors used incorrect and un-researched information when referring to the 1955 mine explosion. They acknowledge the error and have produced this Cameo to rectify the mis-information.

10th Battalion Argyll & Sutherland Highlanders, 1914-1919.
Lieutenant-Colonel Herbert G. Sotheby, D.S.O., M.V.O. Murray, London 1931.

Adolph Hitler. John Toland. Doubleday & Co., New York 1976.

1000 Years of Irish Poetry. Edited by Kathleen Hoagland. Devlin-Adair 1947.

A Deep Cry - Soldier Poets killed in Northern France & Flanders. Anne Powell.
Palladour 1993.

A Sergeant-Major's War. Ernest Shephard. Crowood Press 1988.

Bright Armour: Memories of Four Years of War. Monica Salmond. Faber& Faber 1935.

Diana Cooper - The Rainbow Comes and Goes. Rupert Hart-Davis 1958.

Fifty Years of Eton. Hugh Macnaghten. Allen & Unwin 1924.

For Remembrance. A. St. John Adcock. Hodder & Stoughton.

Gilbert Talbot. Printed for Private Circulation 1916.

History and Memoir of the 33rd Battalion Machine Gun Corps and of the 19th, 89th,
100th and 248th Machine Gun Companies. Waterlow Brothers and Layton Limited,
London 1919.

Irish Heroes in the War. John E. Redmond M.P., T. P. O'Connor M.P. and Joseph
Keating. Everett 1917.

Julian Grenfell. Nicholas Mosley. Holt, Rinehart & Winston 1976.

Julian Grenfell. Viola Meynell, Burns and Oates.

Major-General Sir Henry Wilson Diaries Volume 1. Edited by Major General
C.E.Callwell. Cassell and Co. 1917.

My Recollections of Mons and the First Nine Months of the 1914-18 War. Captain
C.O. Lilly, unpublished memoir.

Raymond Asquith Life and Letters. John Jolliffe. Collins 1980.

Sir Douglas Haig's Despatches. J. H. Boraston O.B.E. J.M.Dent & Sons 1919.

The Thirty-Third Division in France and Flanders 1915-1919. Lieutenant-Colonel
Seton Hutchison. Waterlow & Sons Ltd., London 1921

The South Africans in France. John Buchan. T. Maskow Miller, Capetown, 1921.

The A.I.F. in France 1917. The Official History of Australia in the War of 1914-18,
Volume IV. Dr. C. E. W. Bean. Angus and Robertson Ltd., Sydney, Australia 1933.

The Career of Michael Collins with Special Reference to the Anglo-Irish Treaty 1921.
Unpublished M.A. Thesis University of Bristol, P. A. Freeman.

The Children of the Souls. Jeanne Mackenzie/Chatto & Windus 1986.

The Dorsetshire Regiment. Edited by Terry Bishop.

The Duke of Cornwall's Light Infantry 1914-1919. Everard Wyrrall. Methuen & Co.
Ltd., London 1932.

The Fine Fighting of the Dorsets. Major-General A. L. Ransome C.B., D.S.O., M.C.
Henry Ling 1956.

The Grenadier Guards in the Great War. Lieutenant-Colonel The Right Honourable Sir
Frederick Ponsonby. MacMillan & Co. Ltd., London 1920.

The History of the 1st Regiment R.I.R. 16. Dr. F. Solleder. Munich 1932.

The History of the 9th (Scottish) Division. John Ewing M.C. John Murray,
London 1921.

The History of the Cheshire Regiment in the Great War 1914-1918. Arthur
Crookenden. W. H. Evans Sons & Co. Ltd., Chester.

BIBLIOGRAPHY

The History of the Dorsetshire Regiment 1914-1919. Henry Ling 1932

The History of the Great War, Military Operations, France and Belgium 1917, Volume II, 7th June-10th November. Brigadier-General Sir James E. Edmonds, C.B., C.M.G. H.M.S.O. 1948.

The History of the Rifle Brigade in the War of 1914-1918.
Reginald Berkeley M.C. The Rifle Brigade Club Ltd., London 1927.

The Irish Guards in the Great War. Rudyard Kipking. MacMillan & Co. Ltd., London 1923.

The Last Summer. Kirsty Mcleod. Collins 1983.

The Memoirs of Lord Chandos. Bodley Head 1962.

The Micks. The Story of the Irish Guards. Peter Verney. Peter Davies, London 1970.

The Official History of New Zealand Division's Effort in the Great War, Volume II, France. Colonel H. Stewart, CMG, DSO, MC. Whitcomb and Tombs Ltd., New Zealand, 1921.

The Old Lie. Peter Parker. Constable 1987.

The Worcester Regiment in the Great War. Captain H. FitzM. Stacke M.C. G. T. Cheshire & Sons Ltd. 1928.

Tunnellers. Captain W. Grant. Grieve and Bernard Newman. Herbert Jenkins Ltd., London 1920.

War Underground. Alexander Barrie. Frederick Muller Ltd., London 1962.

Ypres 1914. German General Staff. Constable and Co., London 1919.

Private Papers. Peter Barton.

Private Papers. David Cohen.

Private Papers. The late Don Forsythe. South Africa.

Private Papers. Mary Ellen Freeman.

Private Papers. Ted Smith.

Private Papers. Tony Spagnoly.

INDEX

INDEX